# Under the Sea

## Coloring Book

Adult Colouring Books

Aryla Publishing 2019

978-1-912675-52-4

www.arylapublishing.com

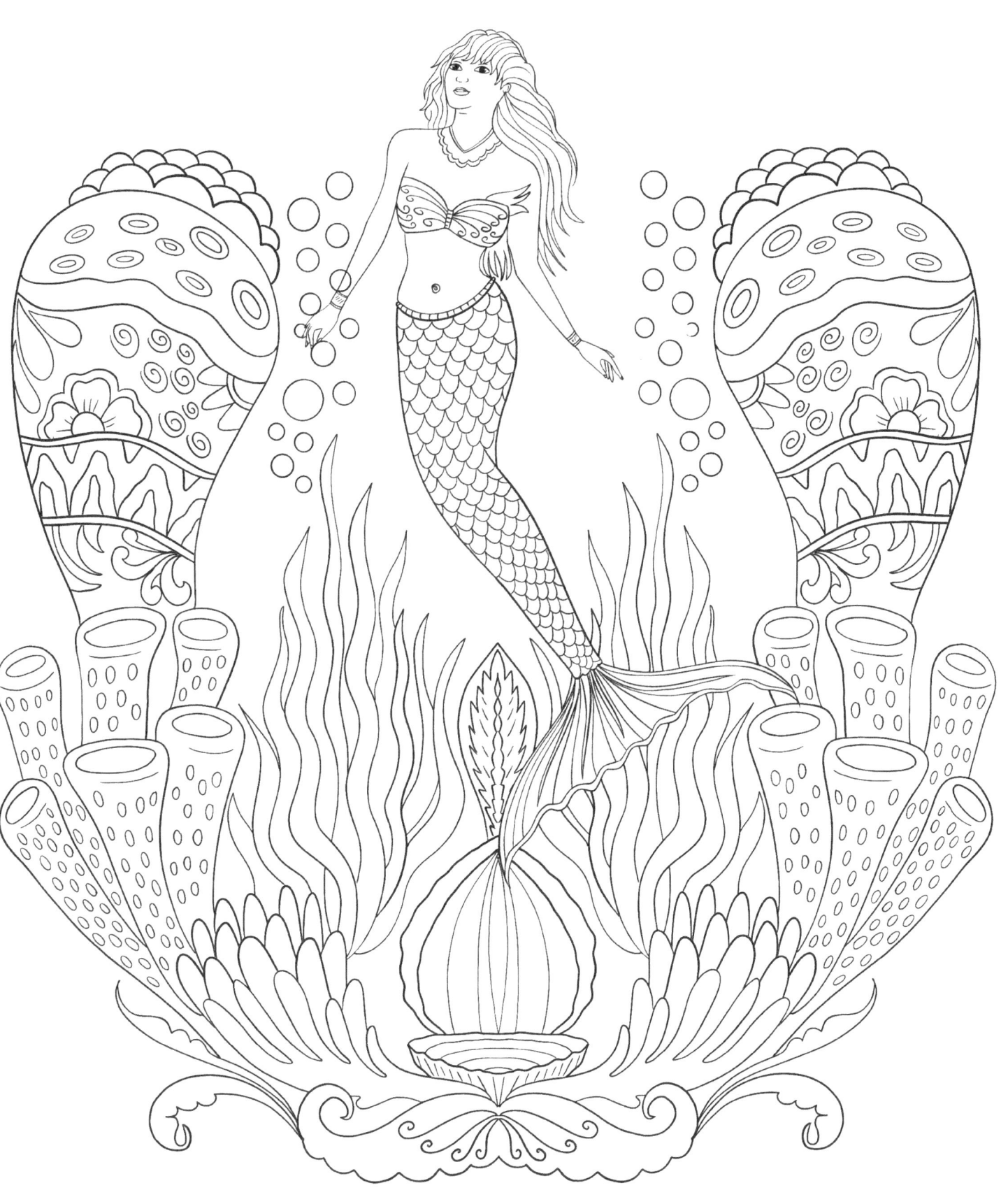

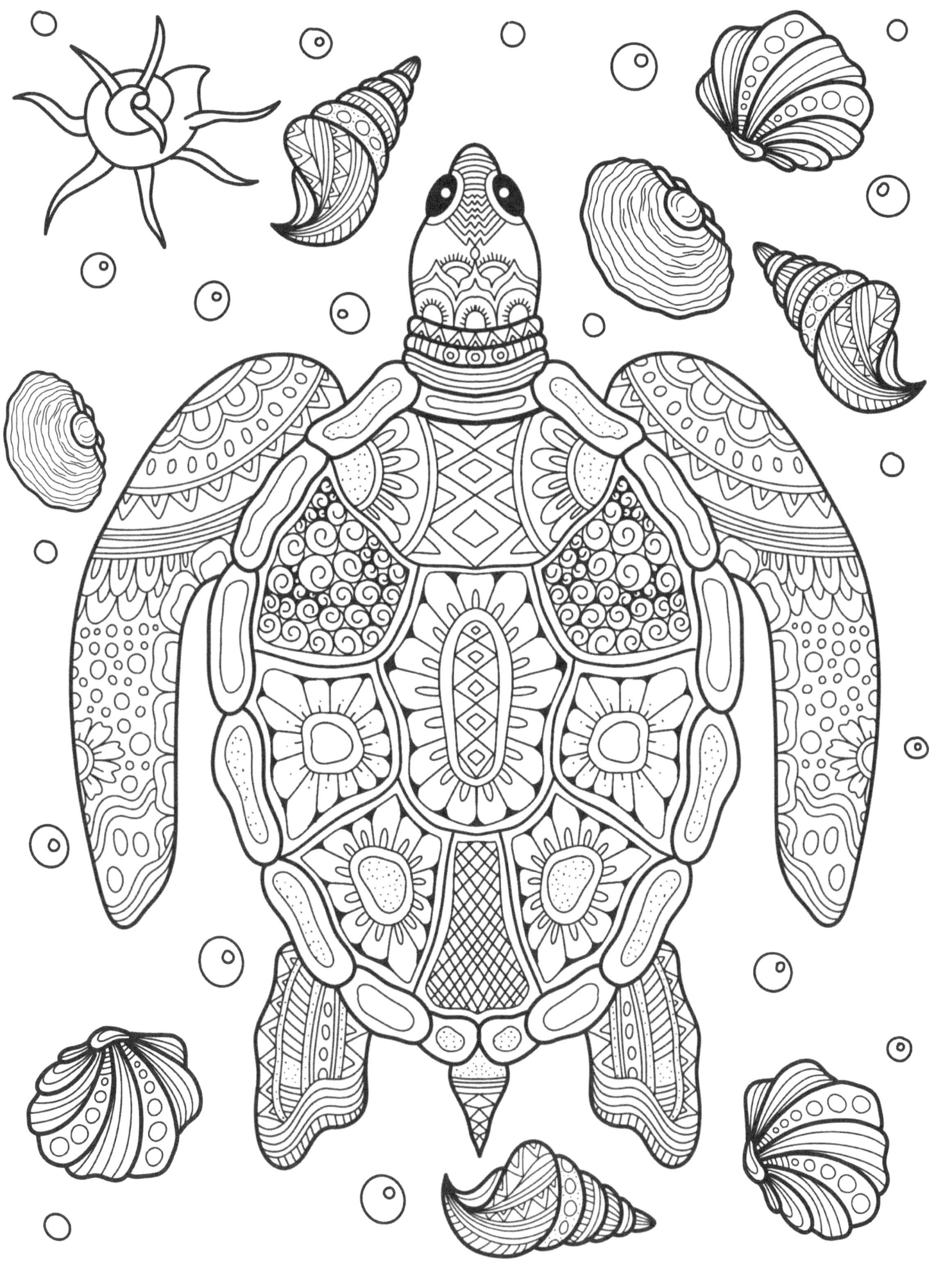

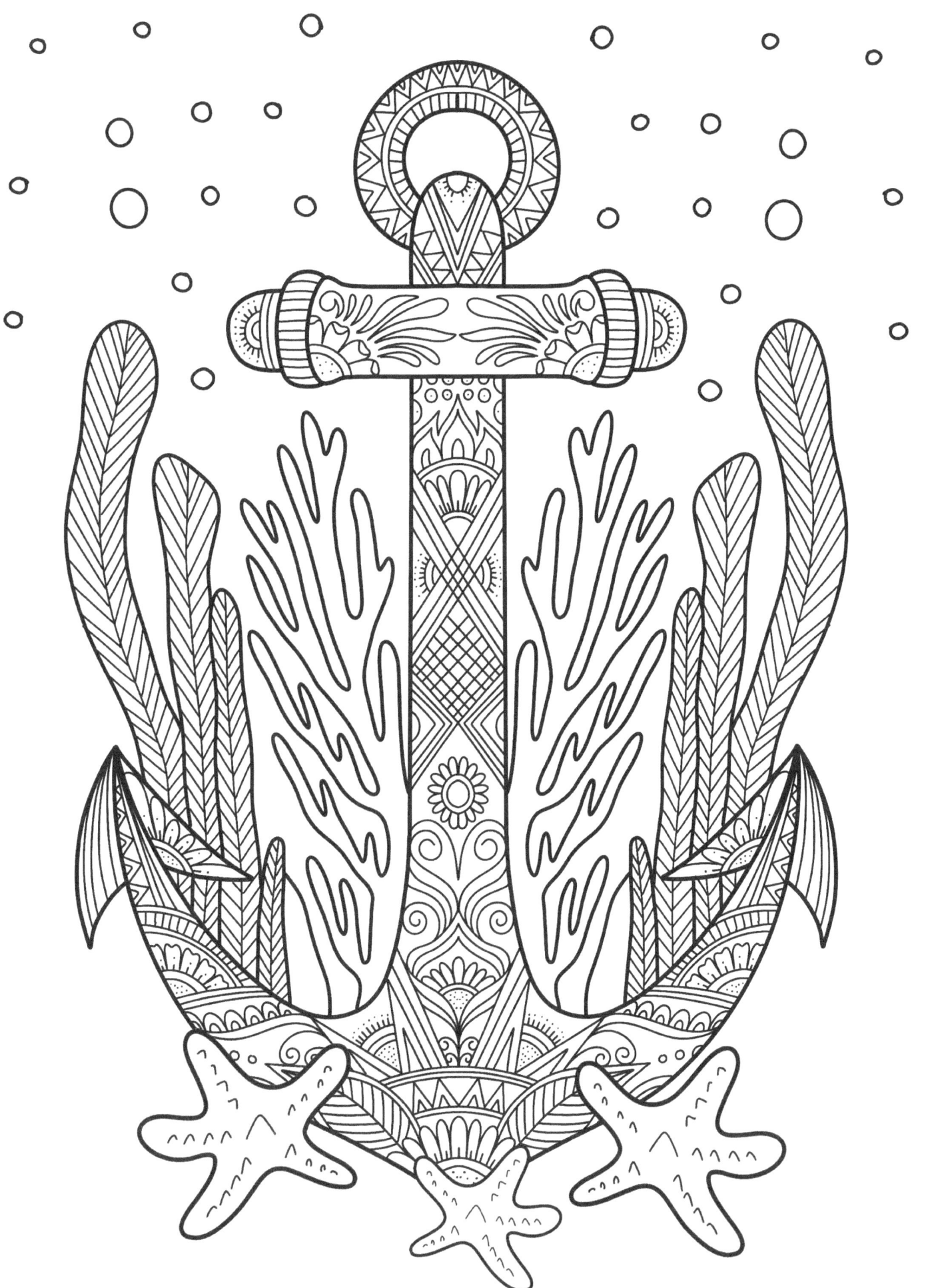

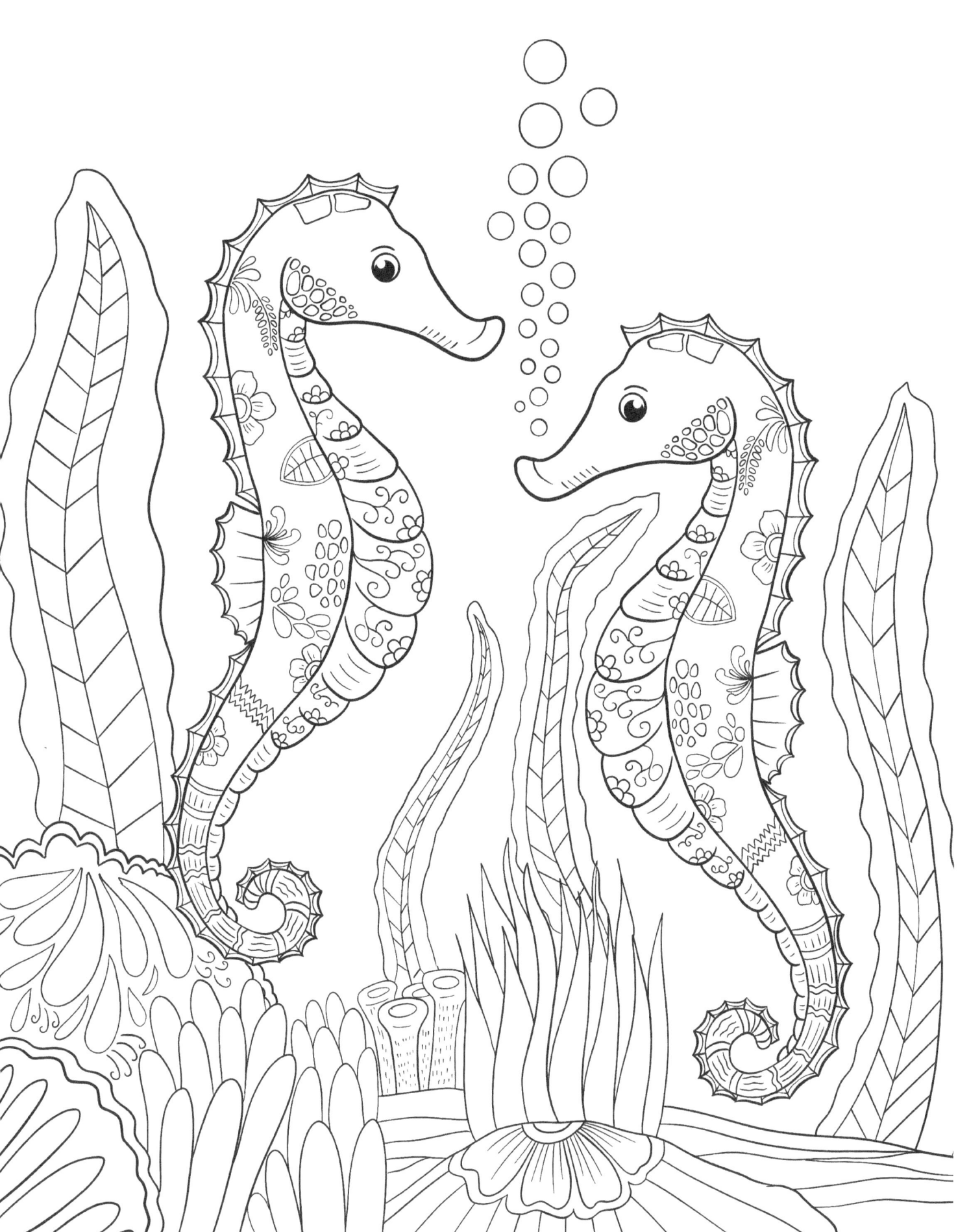

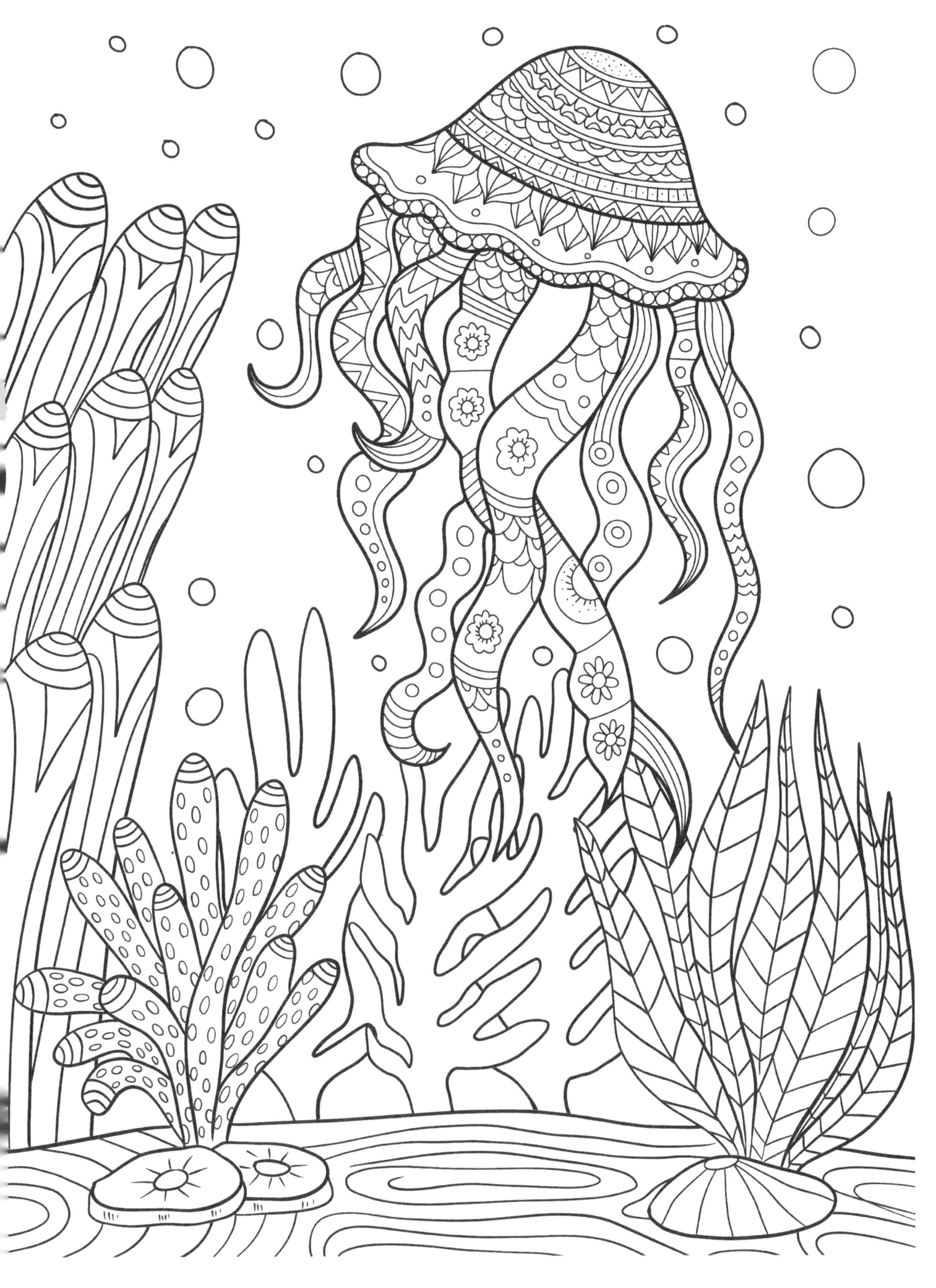

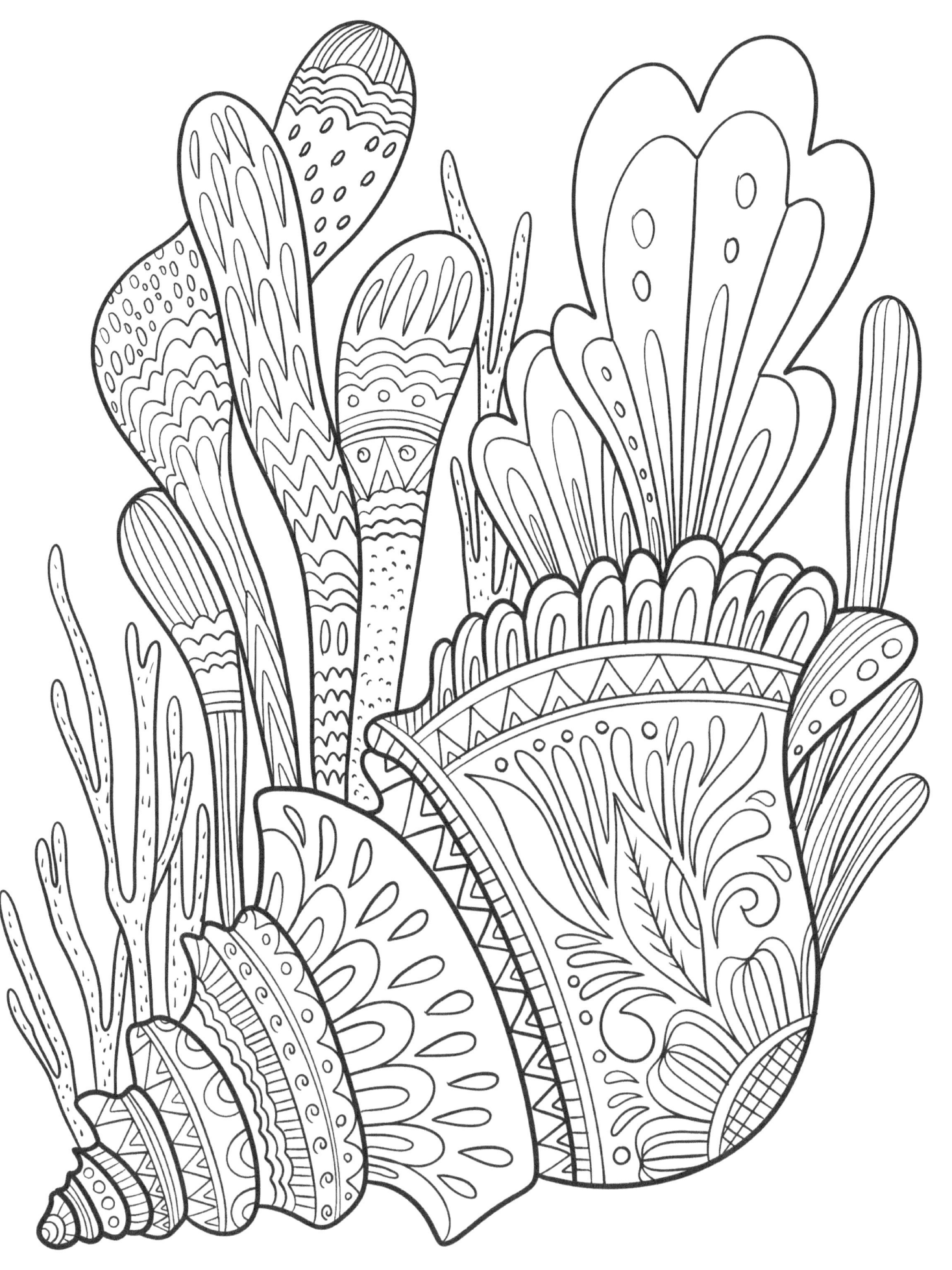

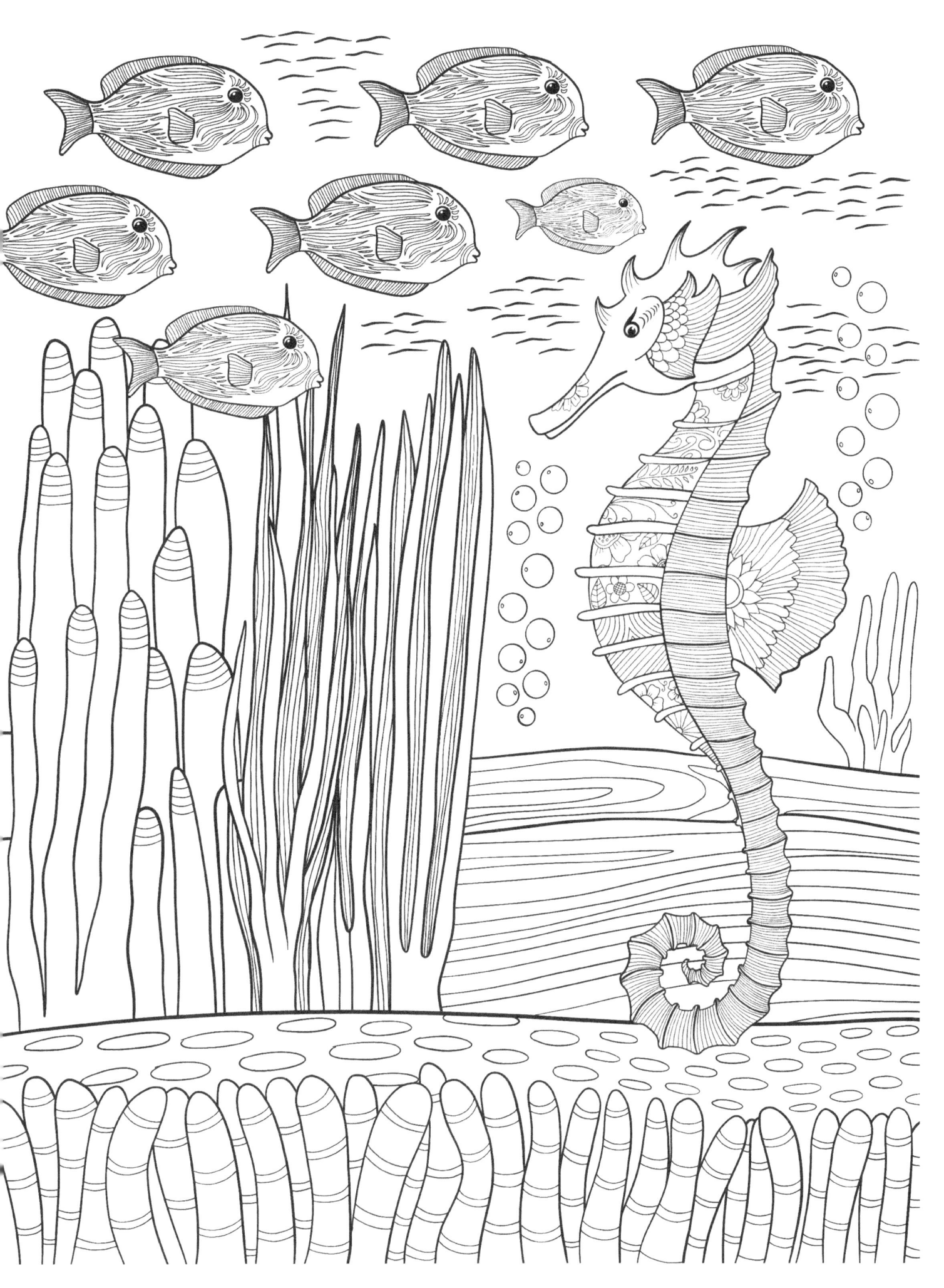

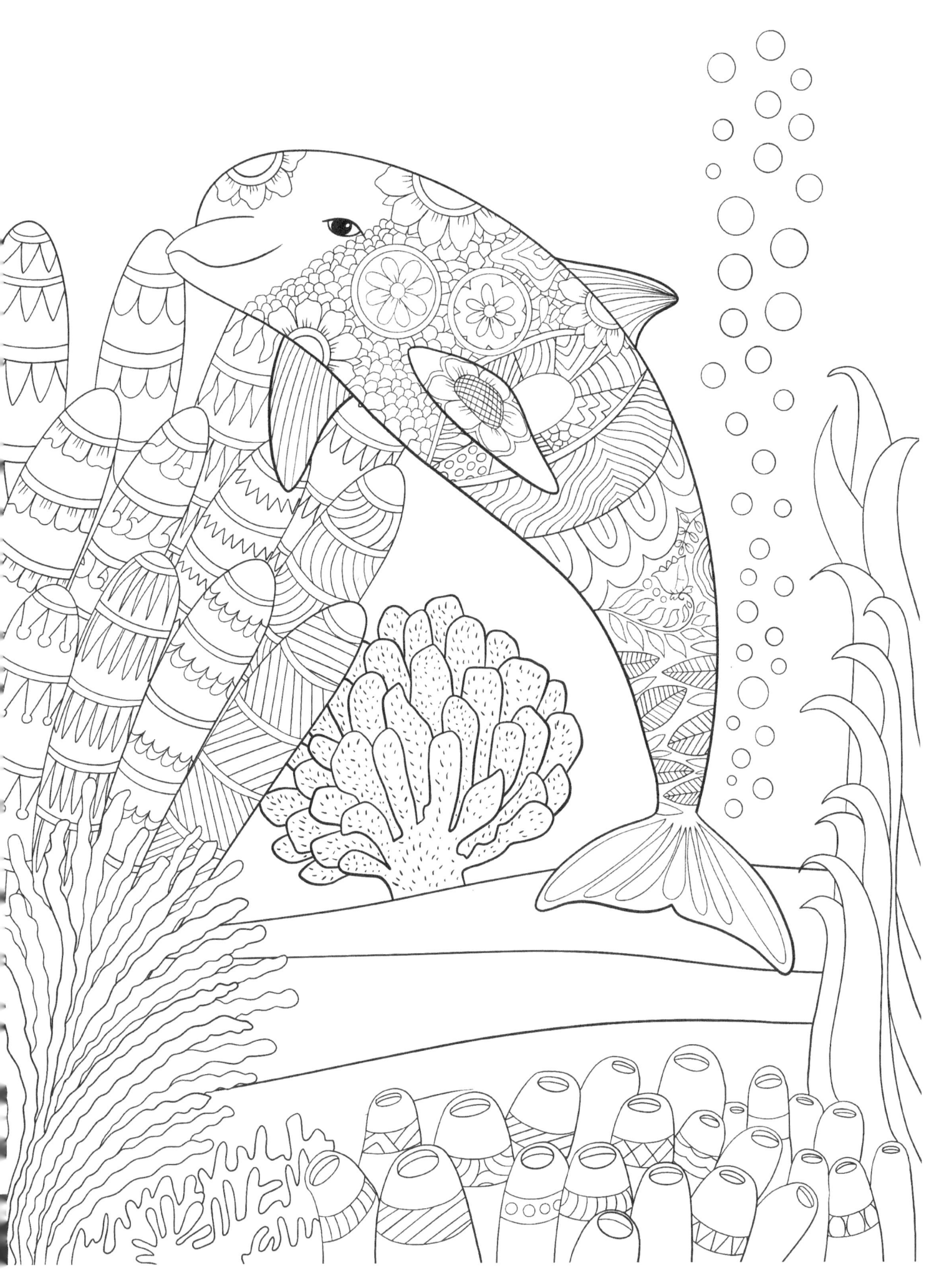

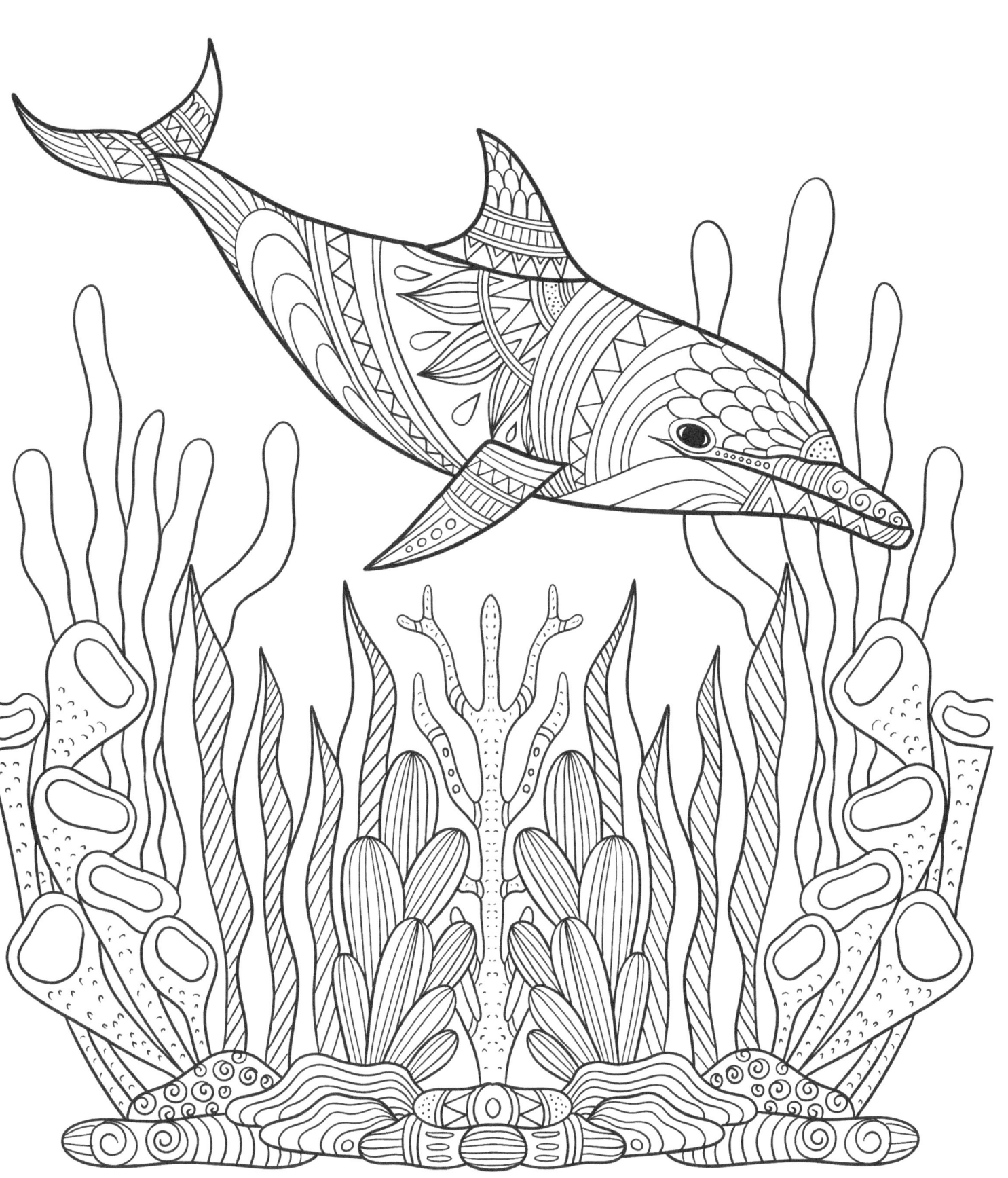

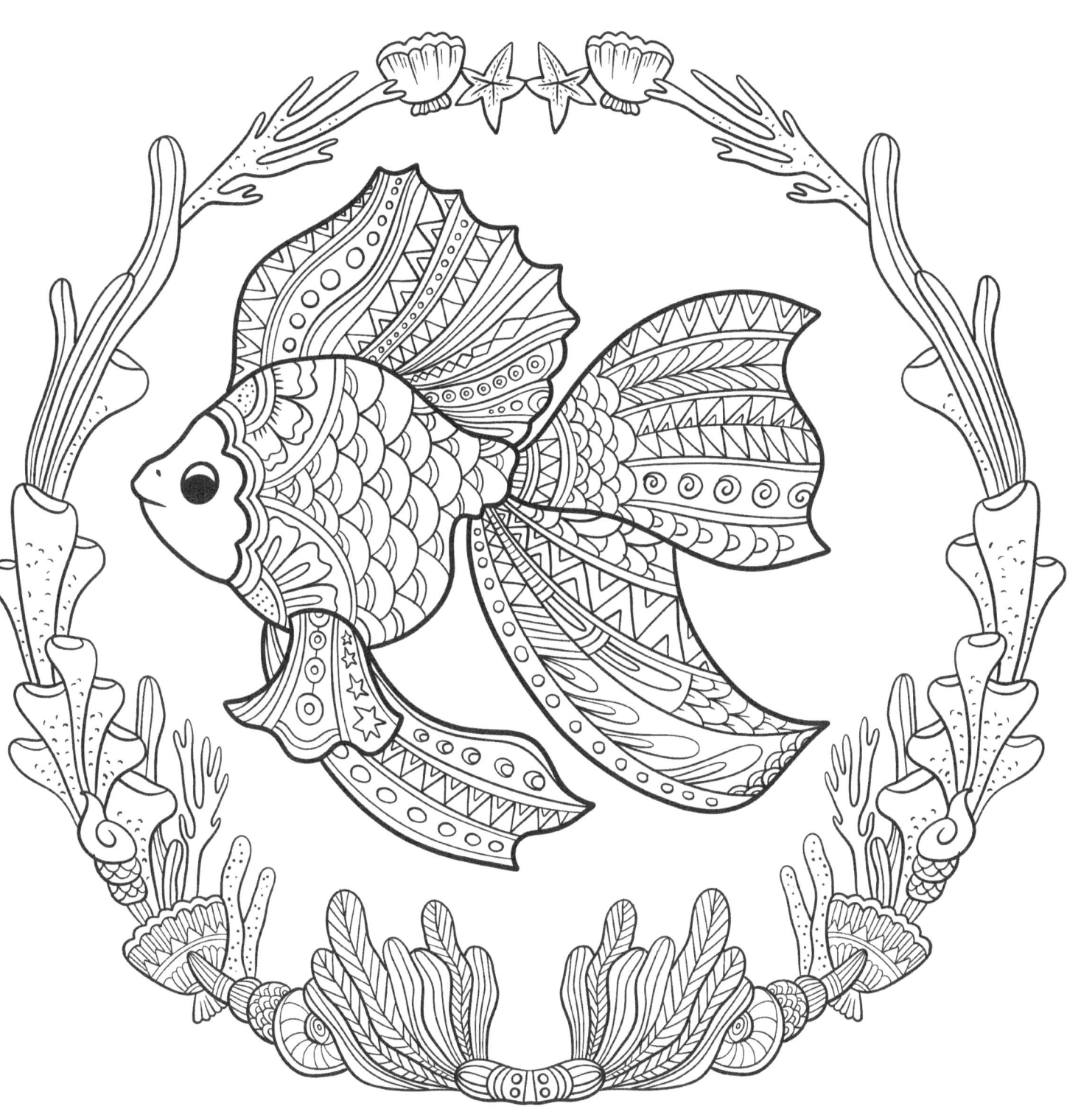

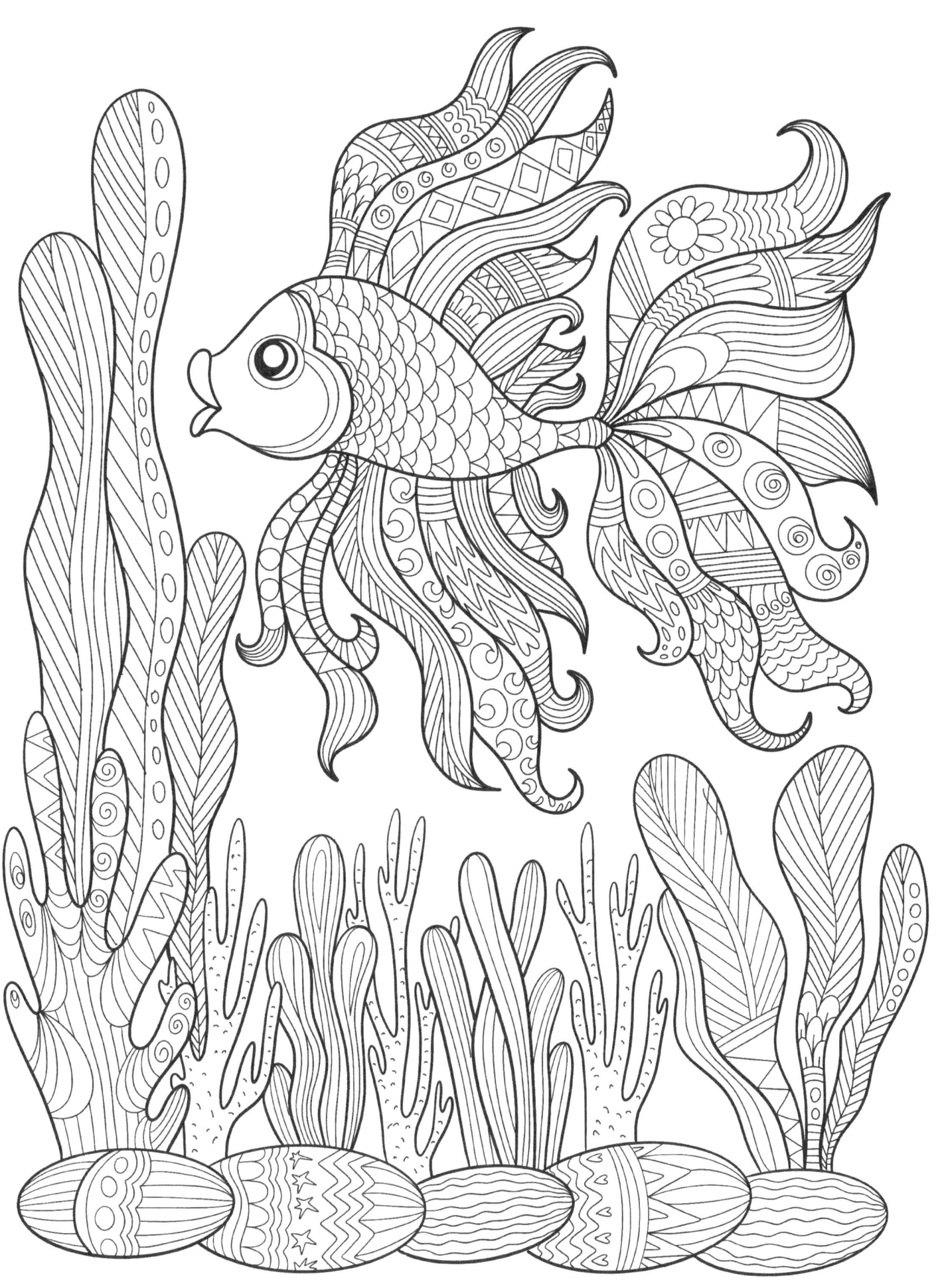

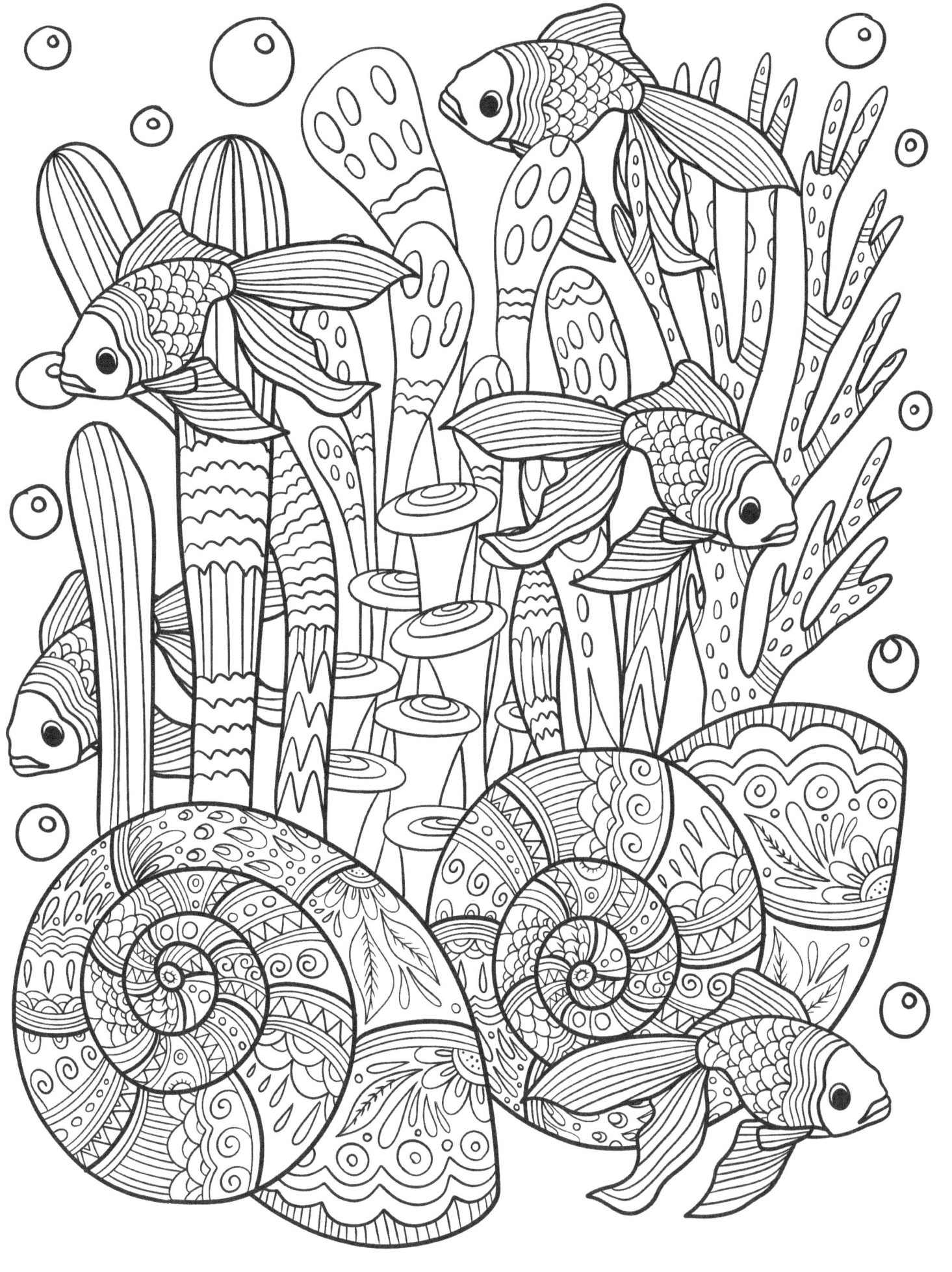

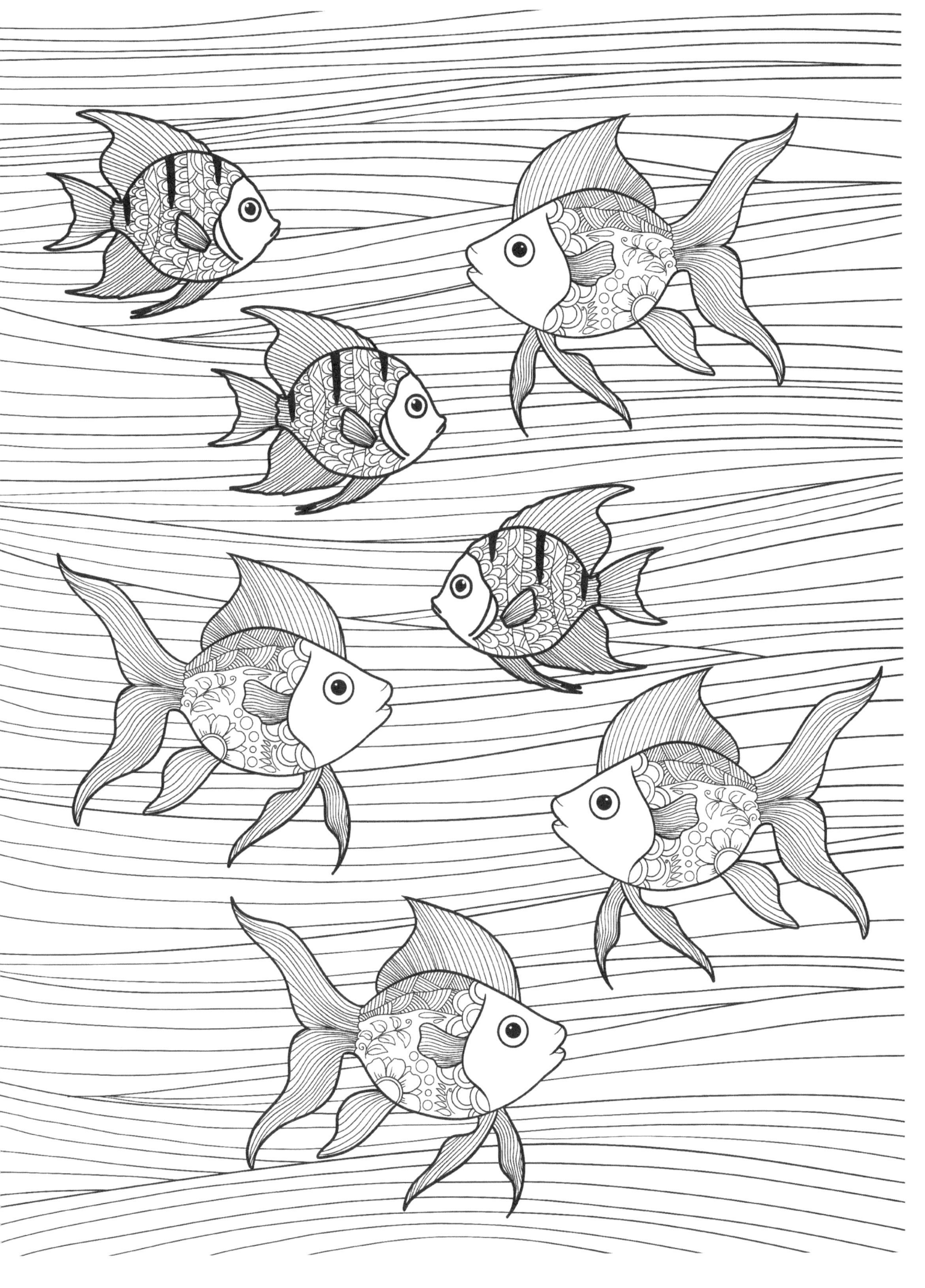

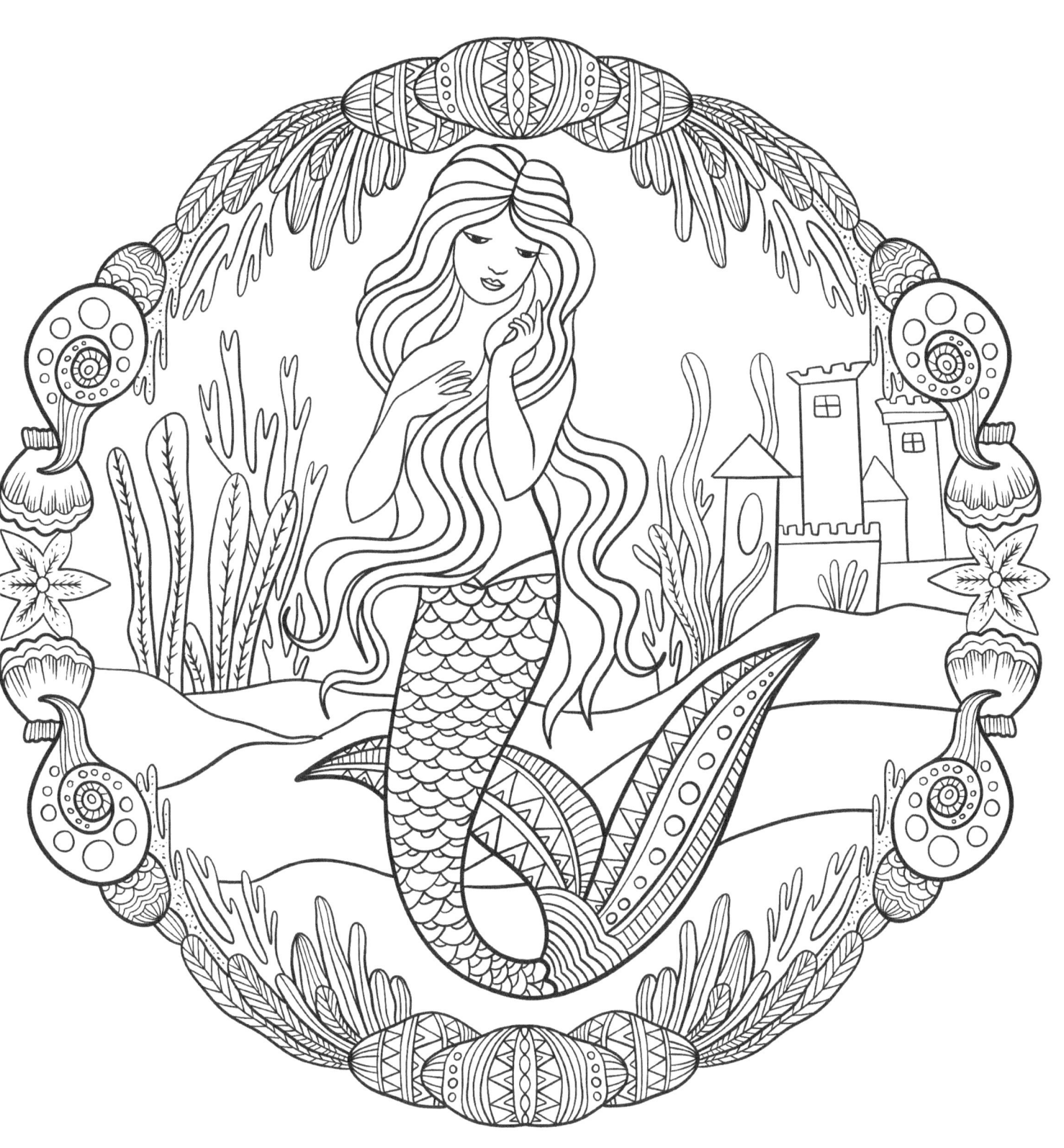

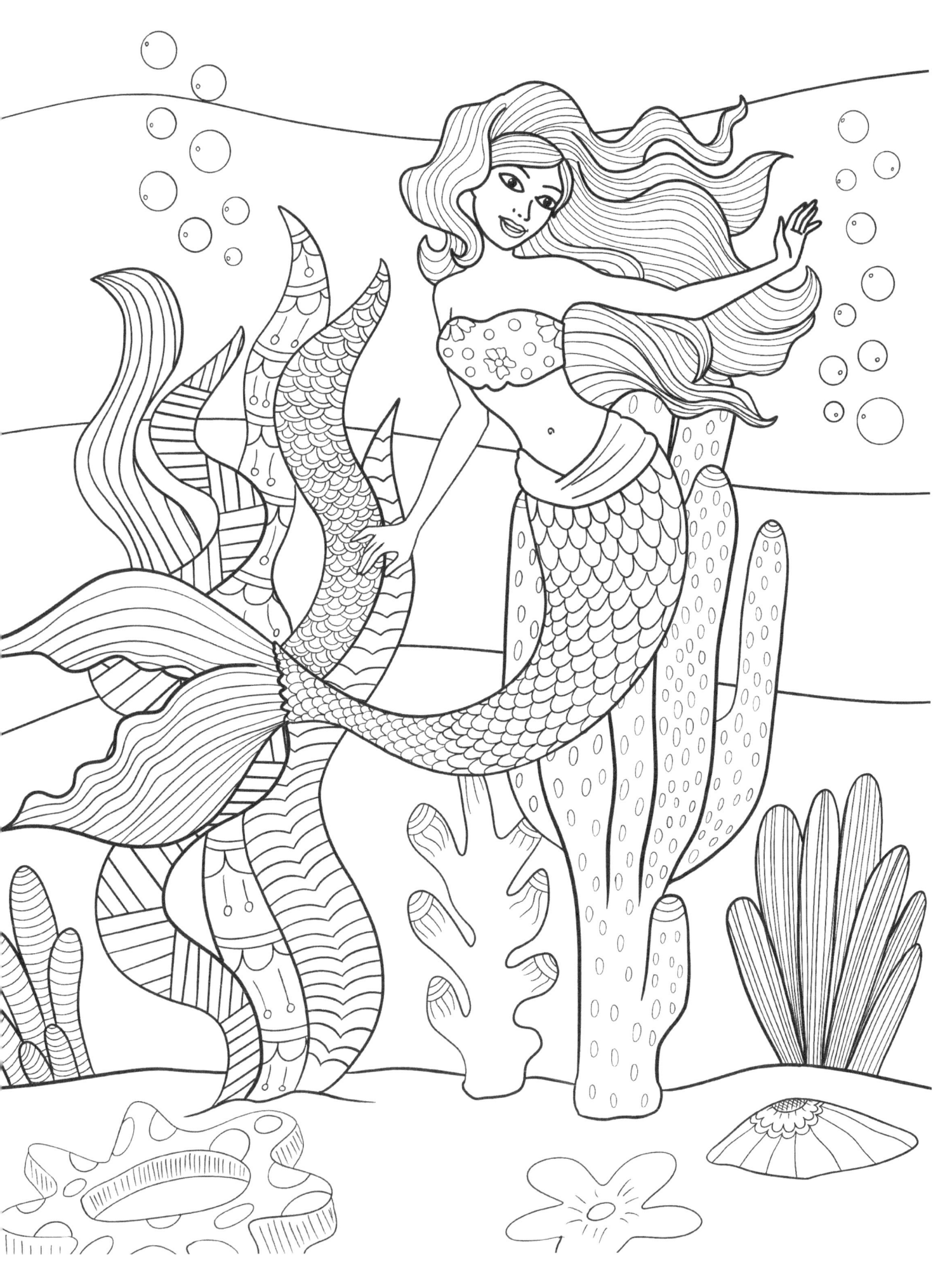

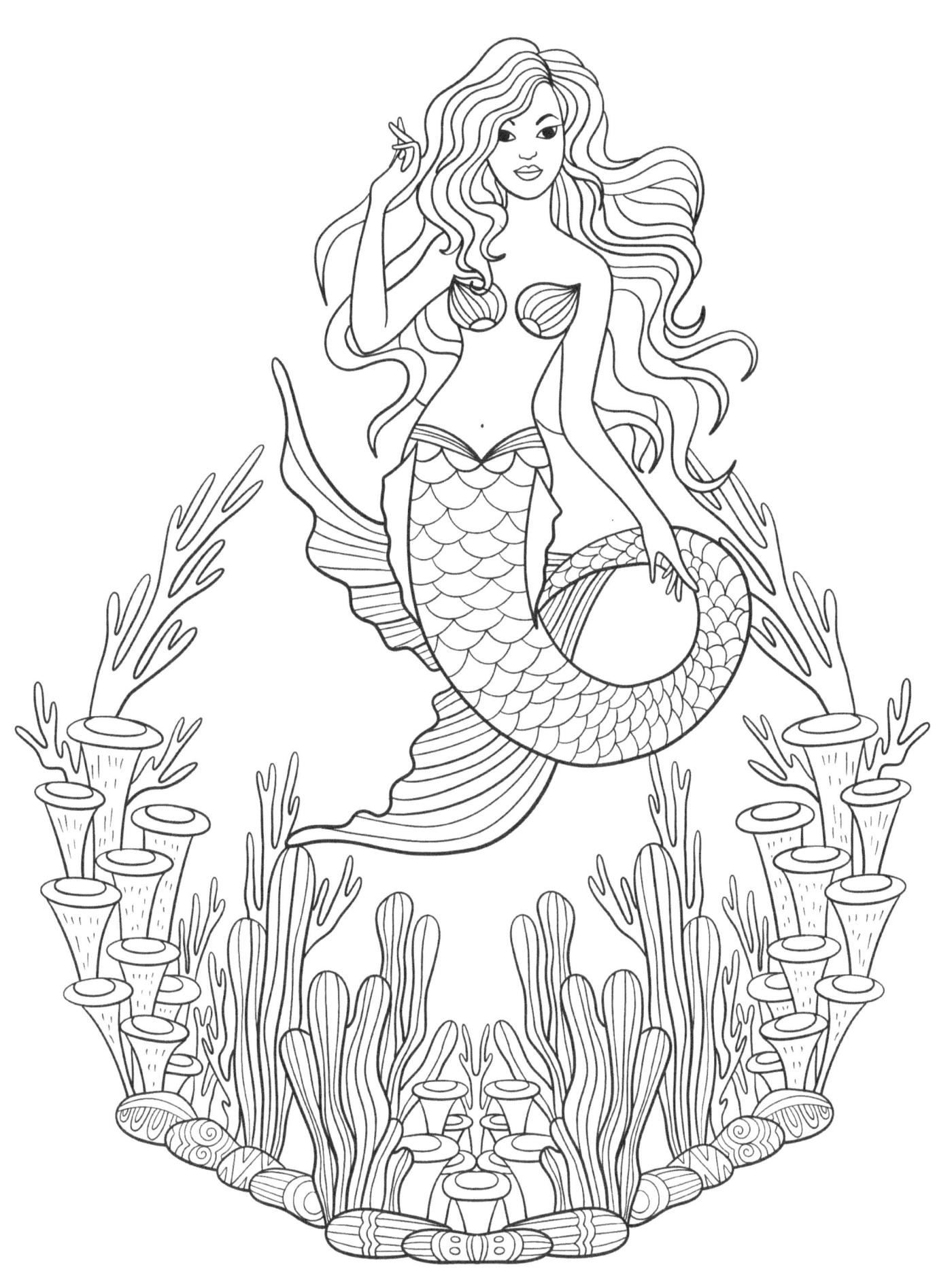

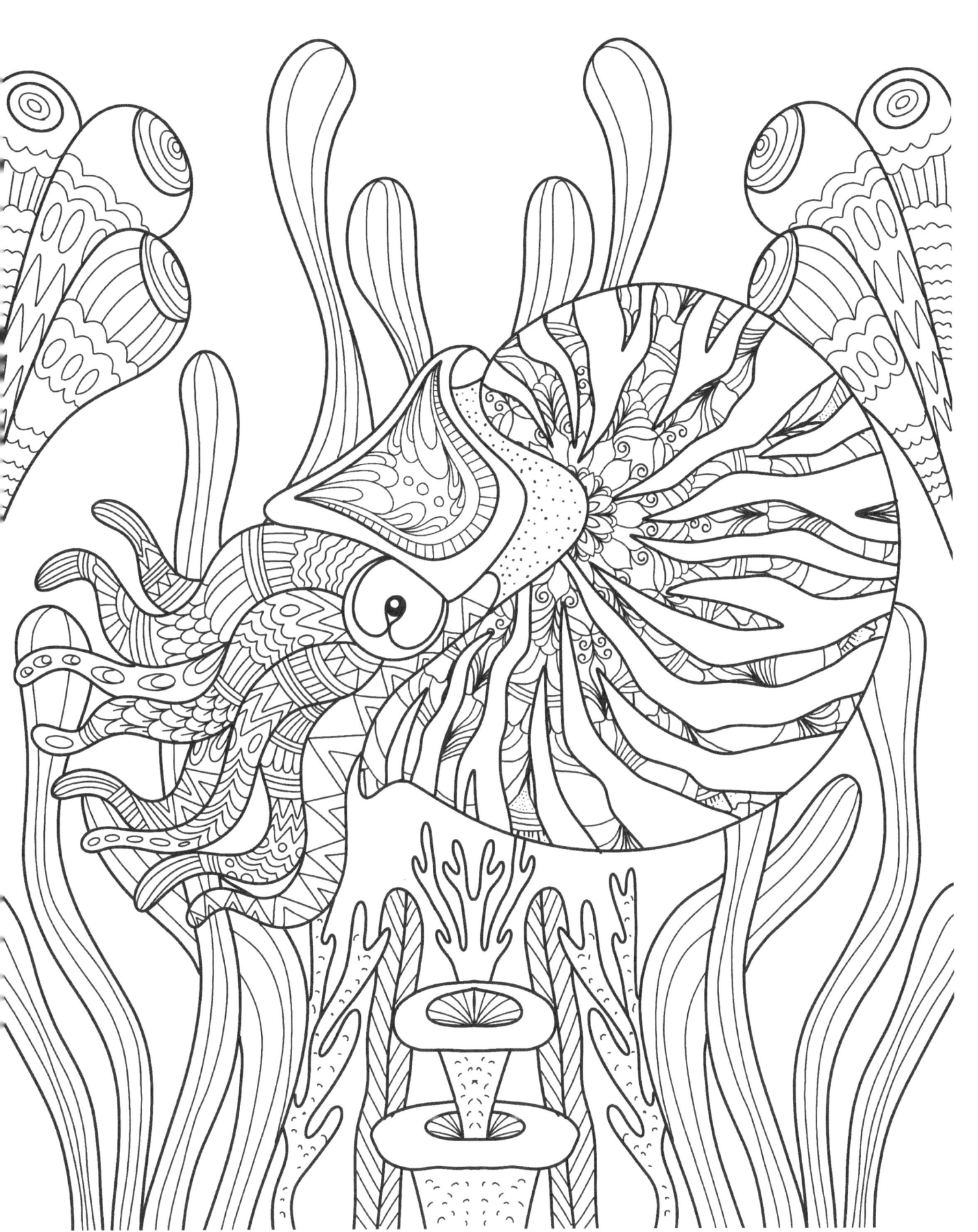

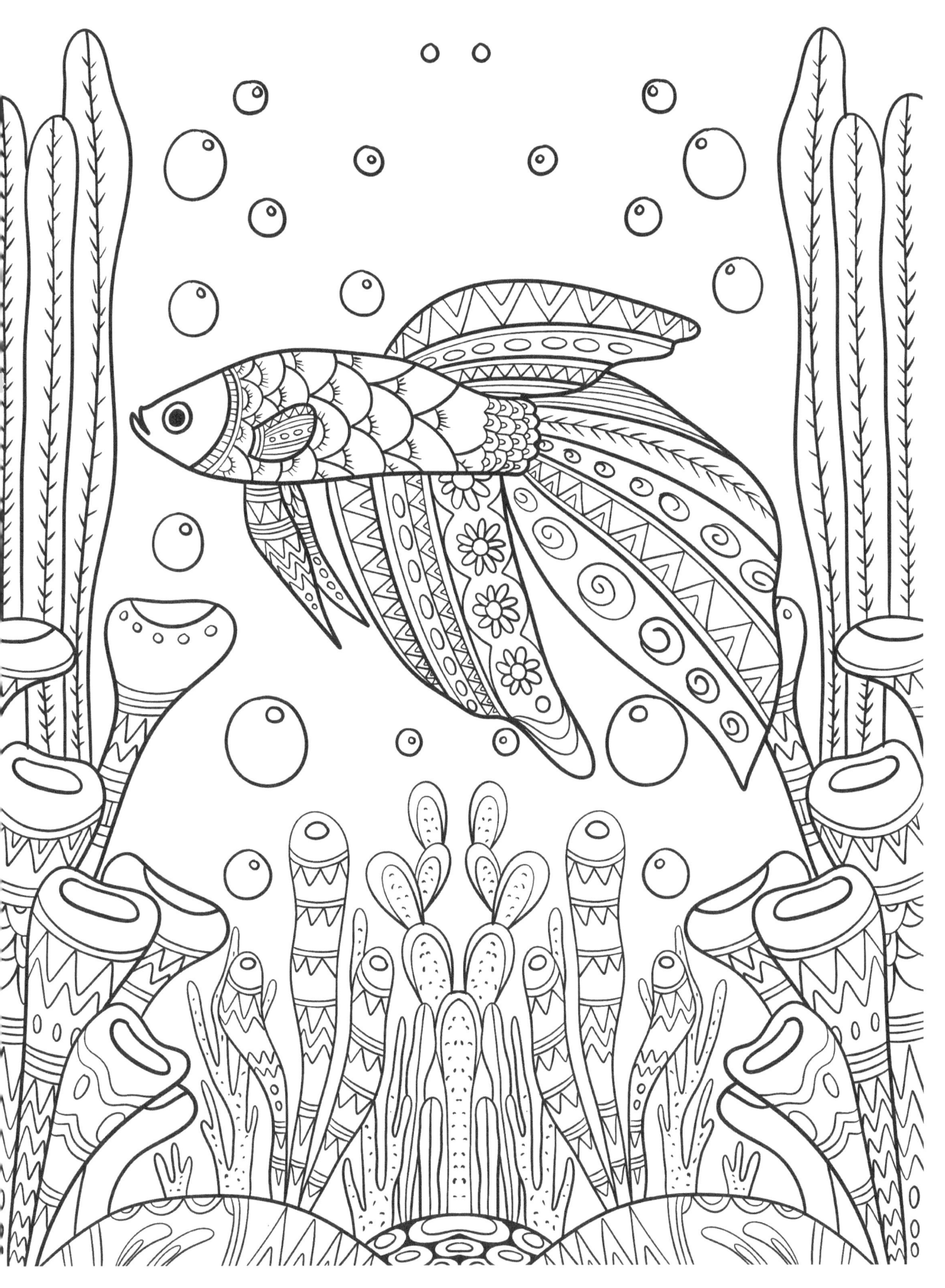

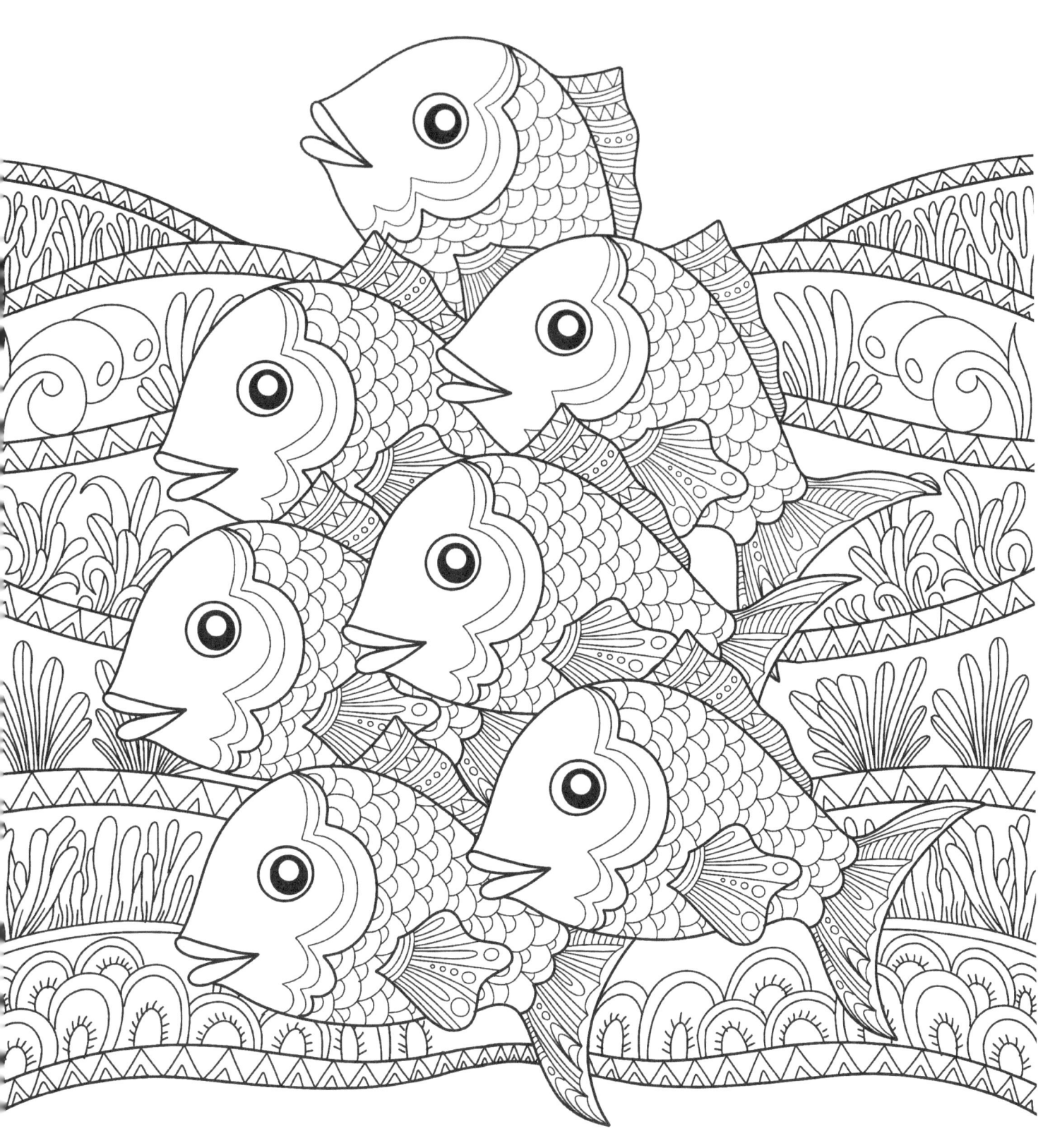

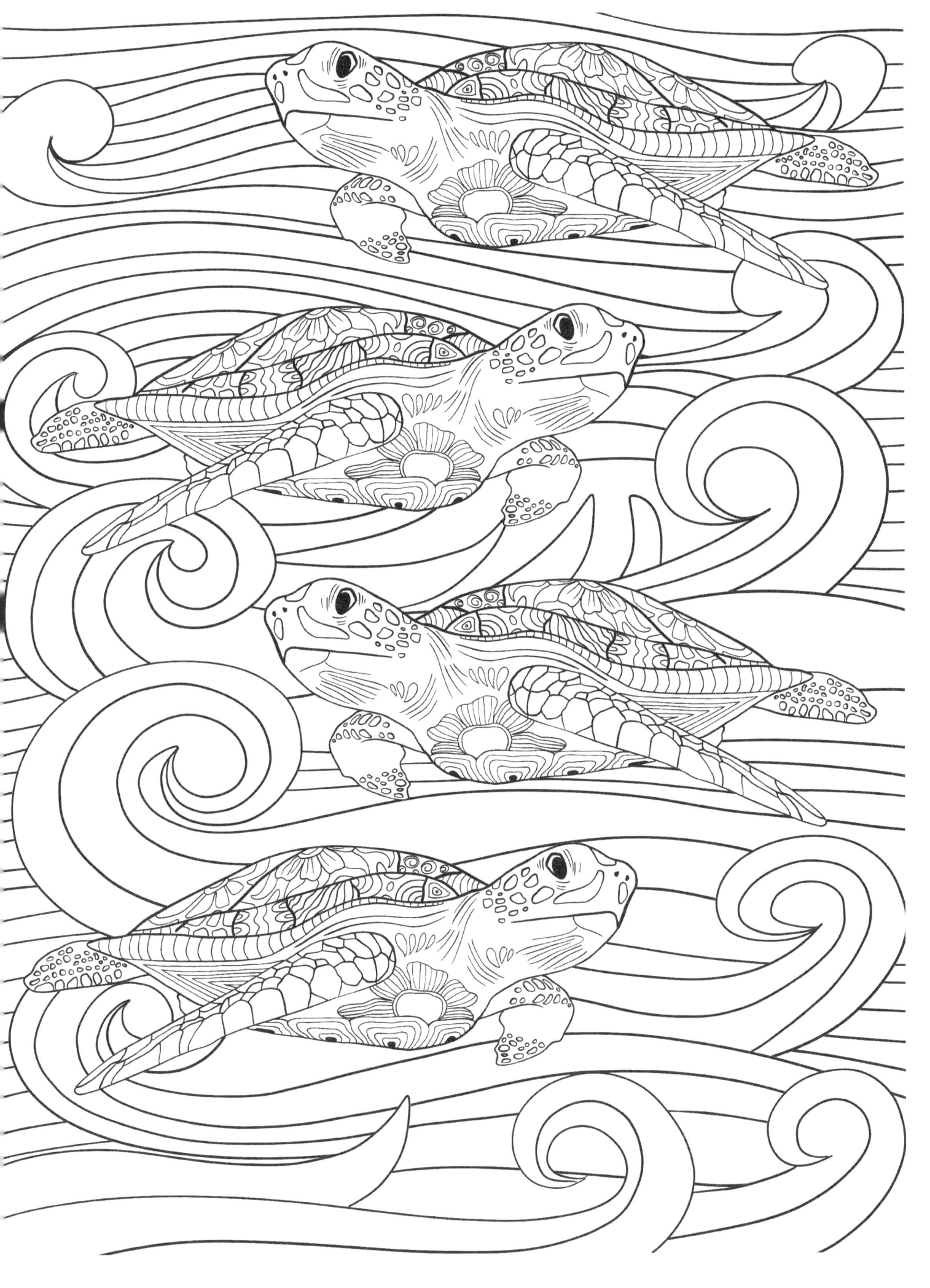

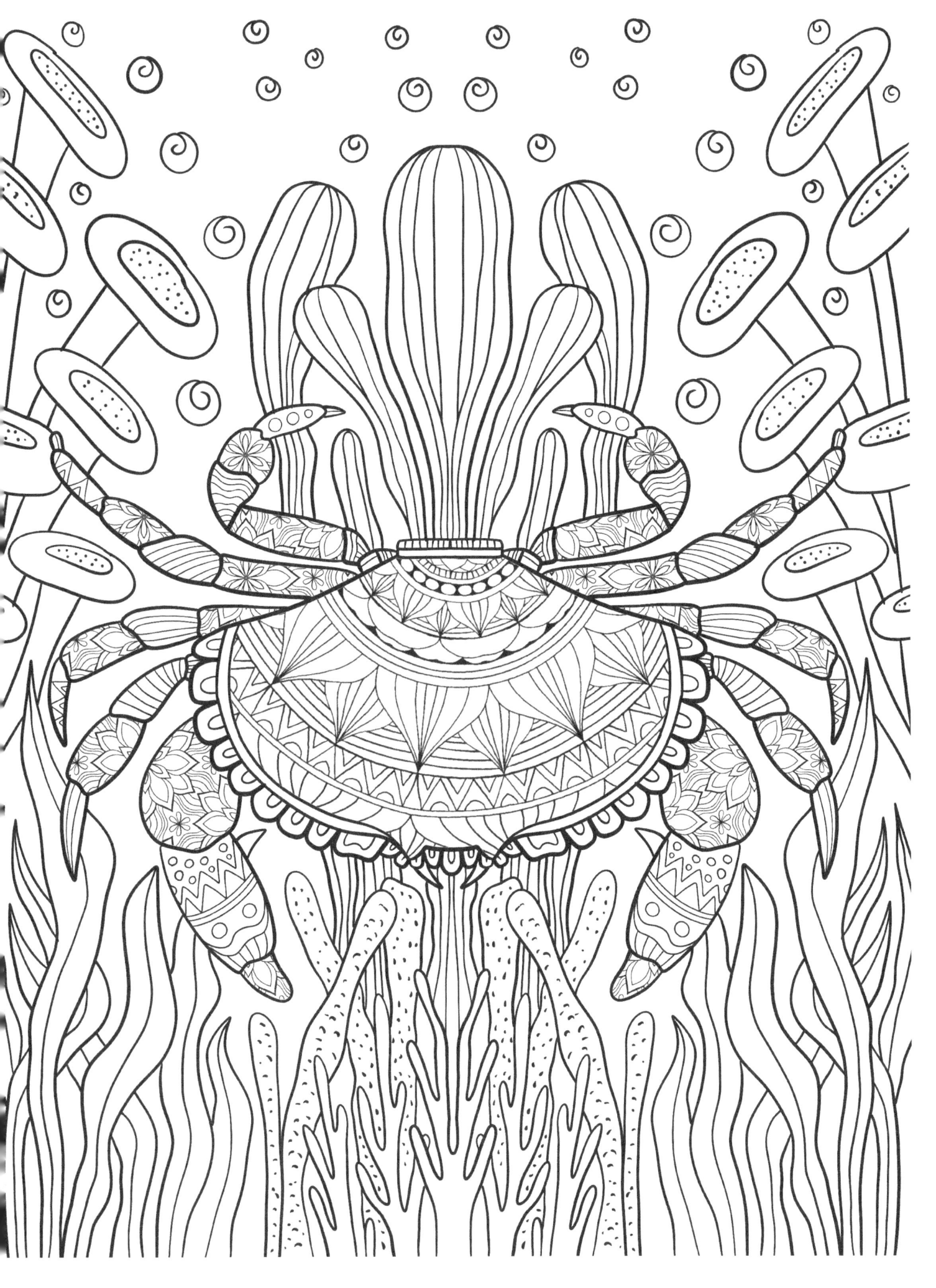

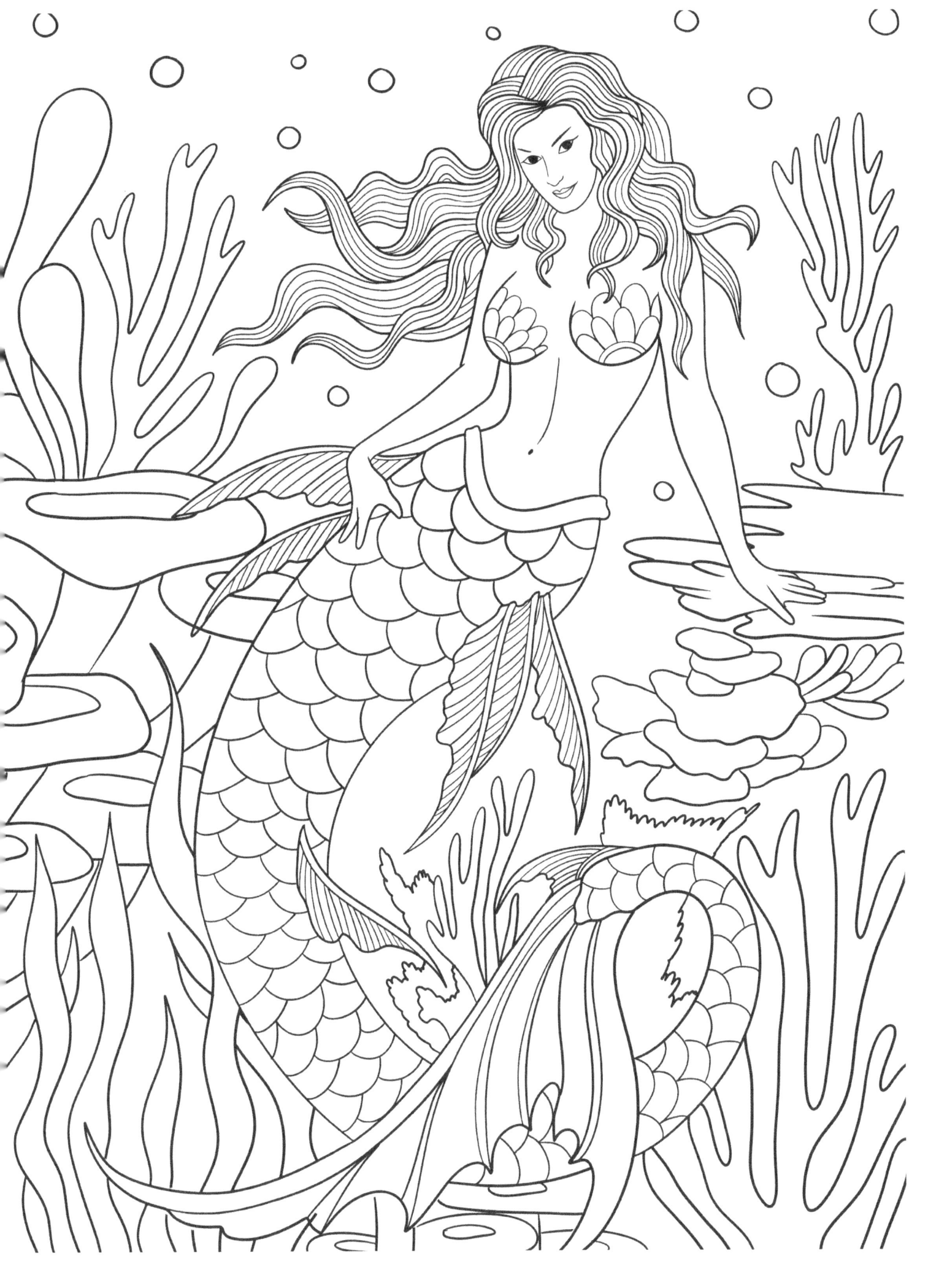

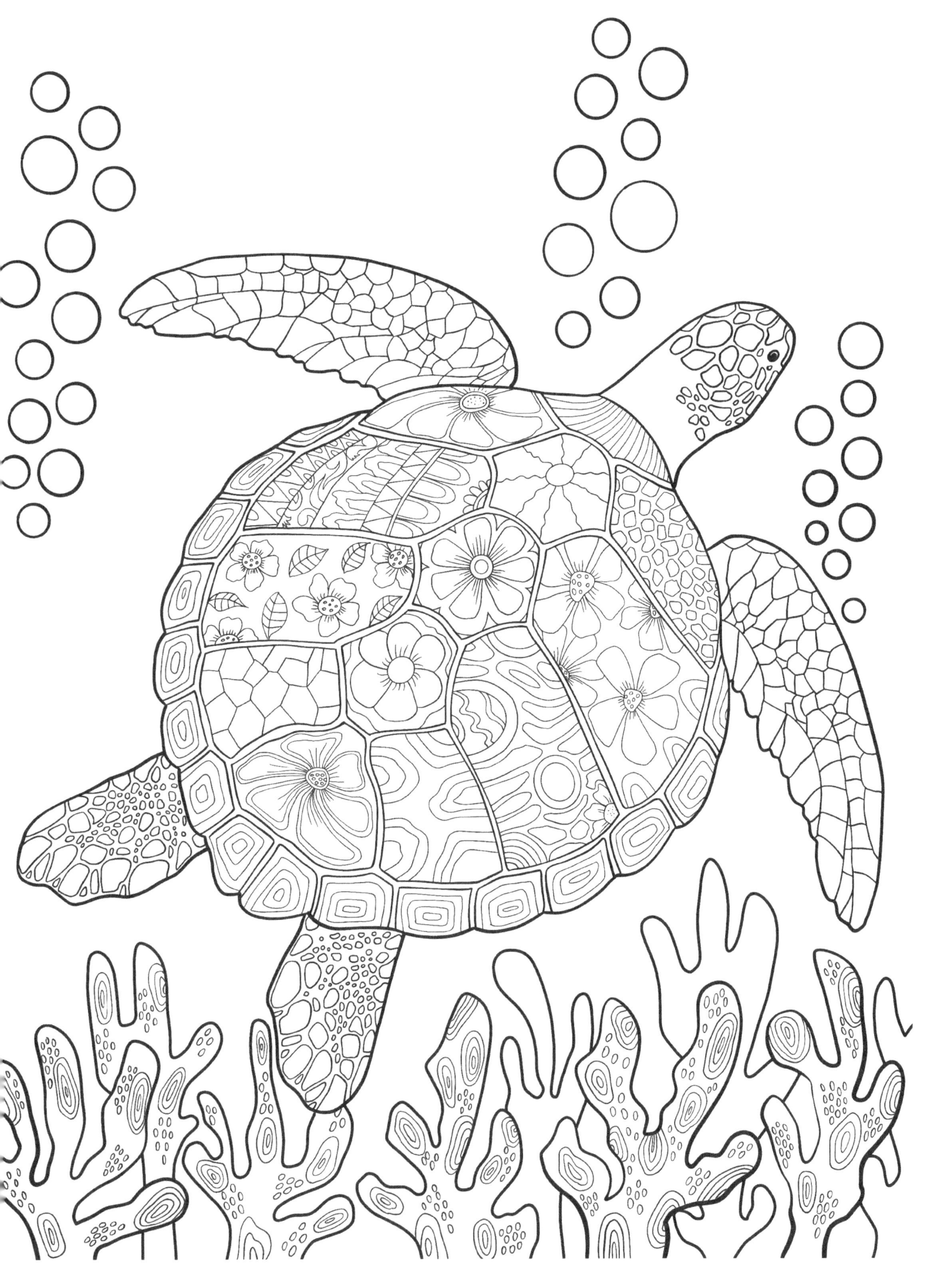

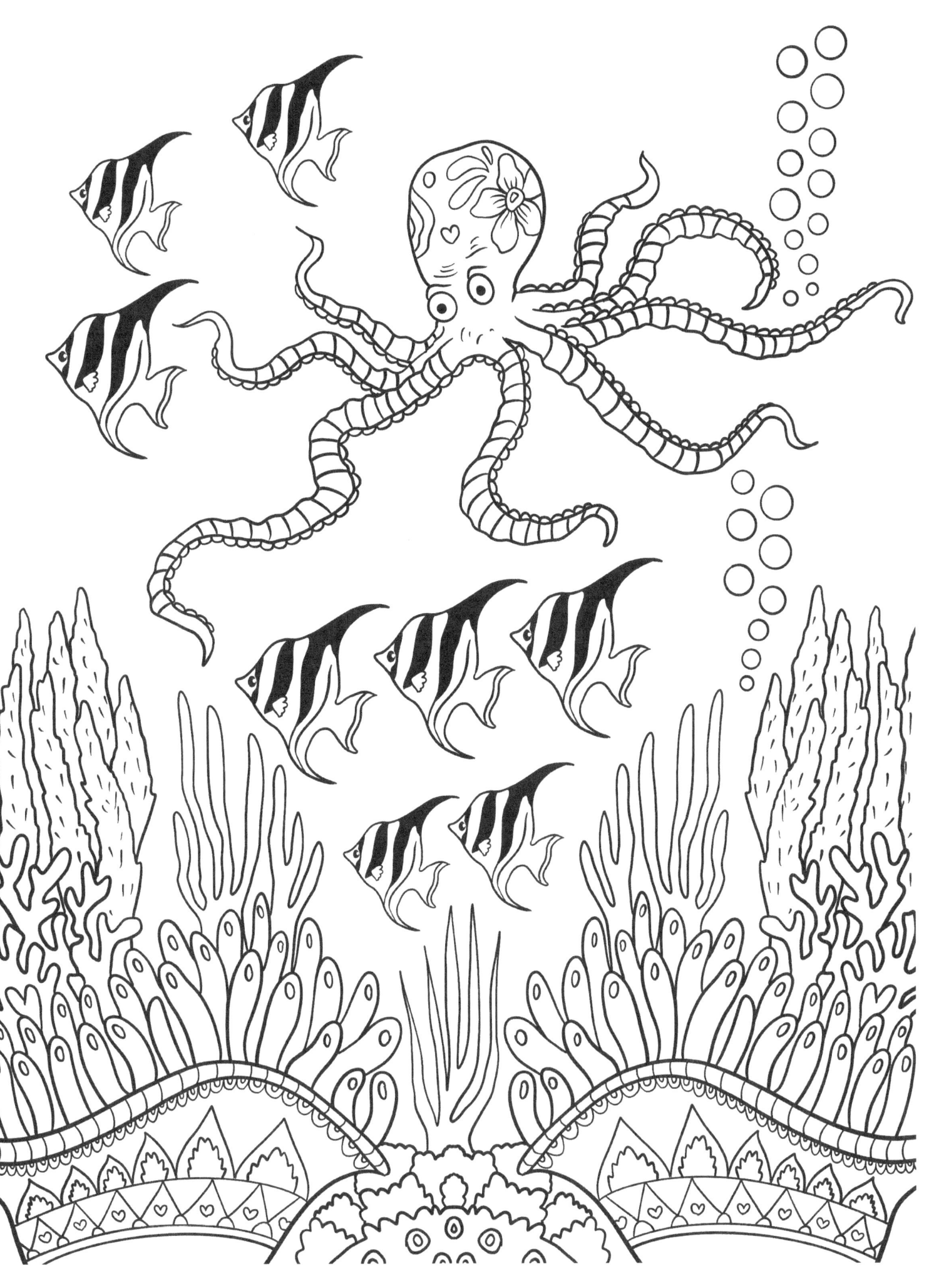

# Other Coloring Books from Aryla Publishing

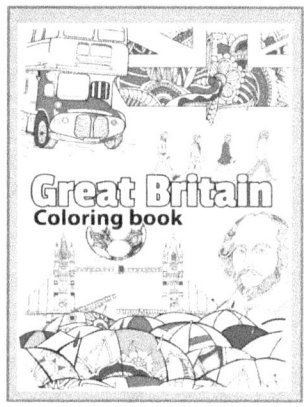
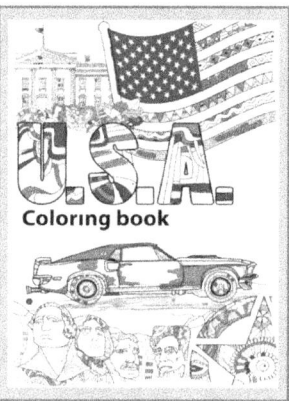
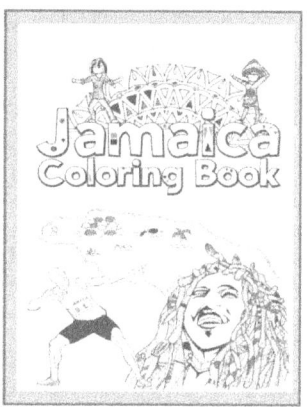
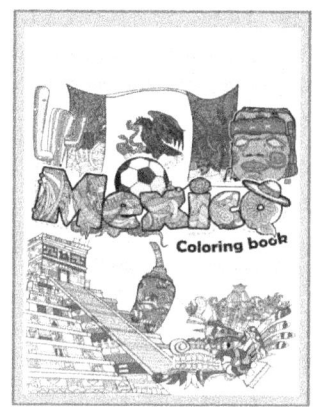

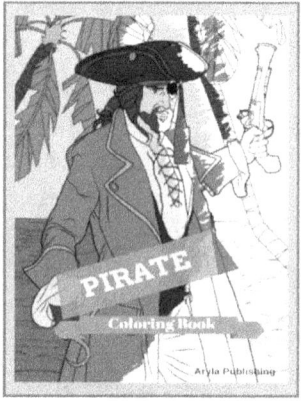
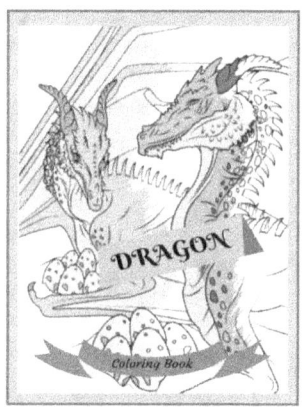
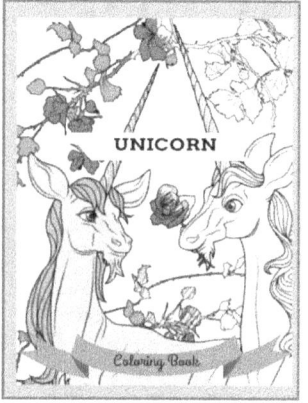
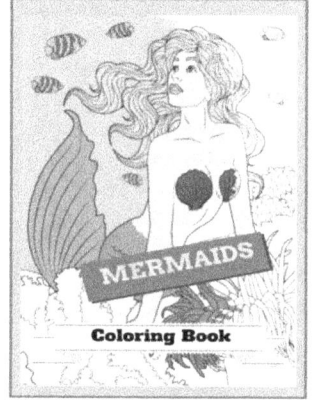

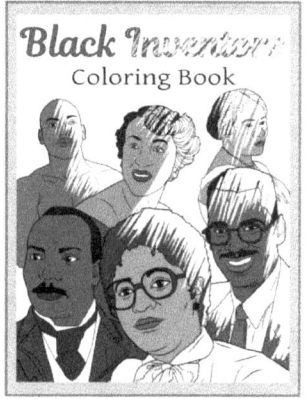
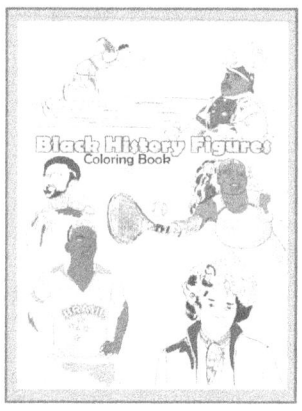
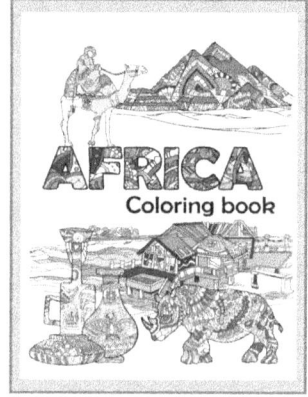
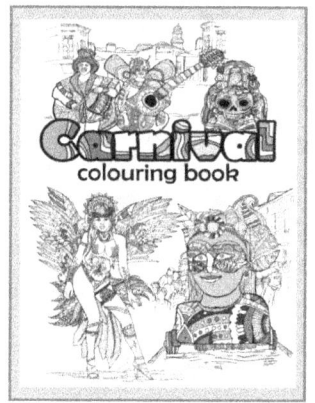

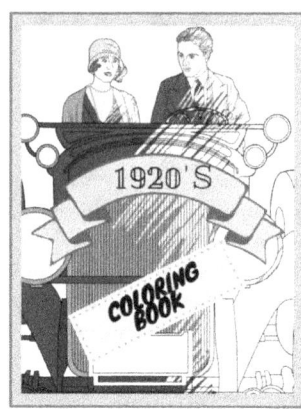
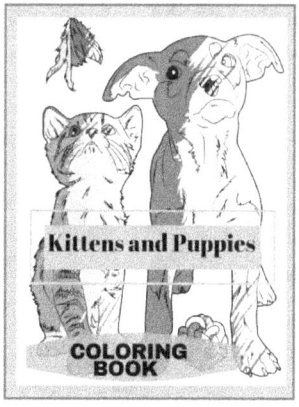
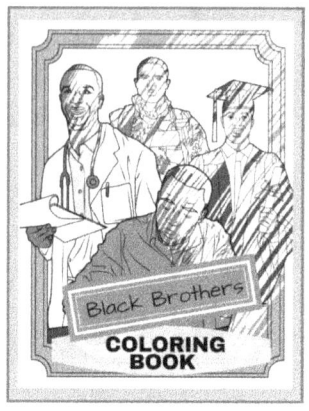
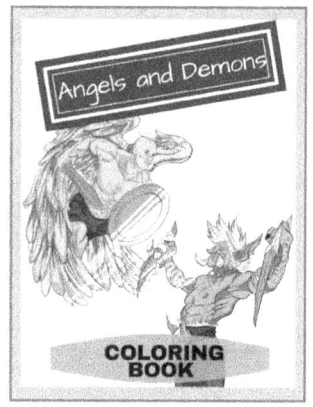

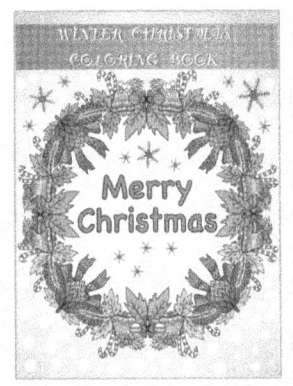
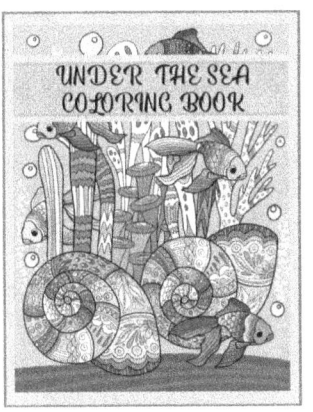
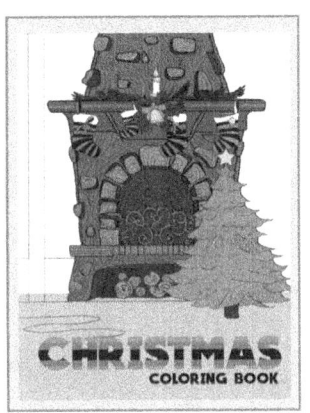
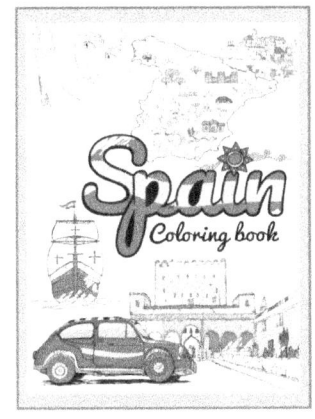
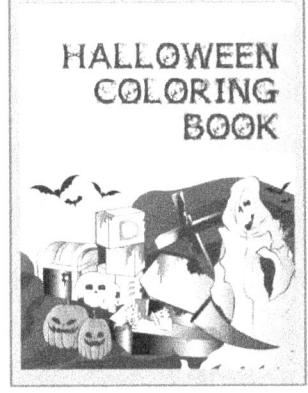
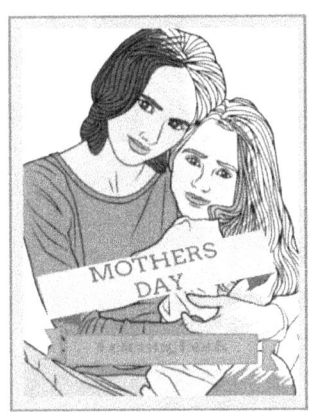
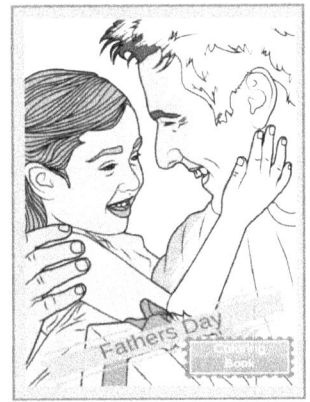
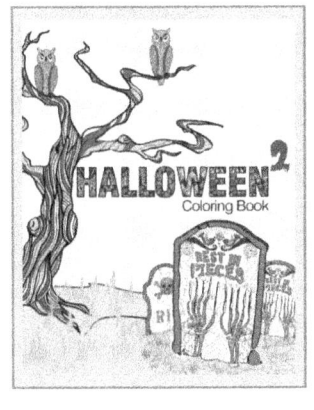
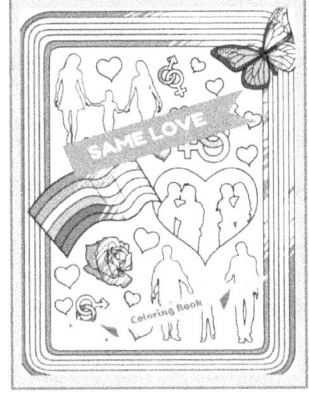
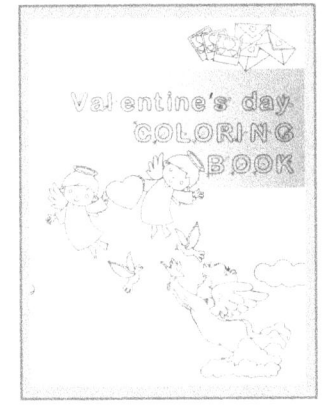
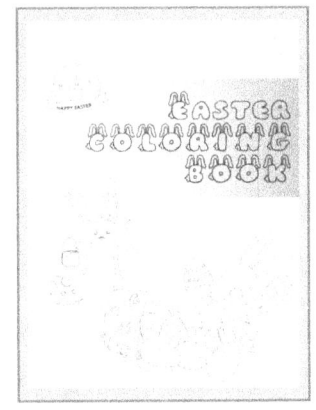
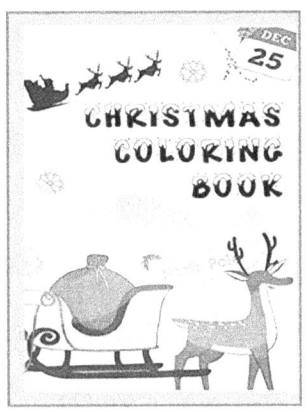
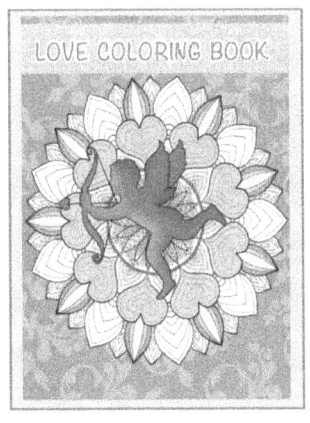
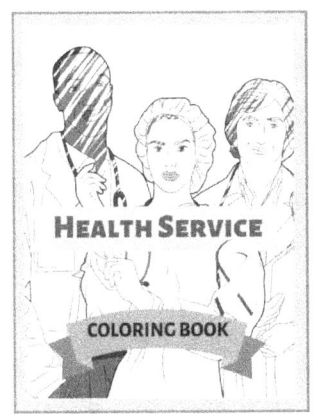
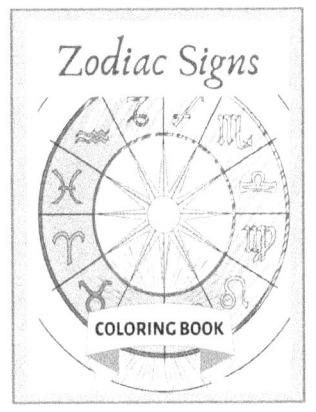
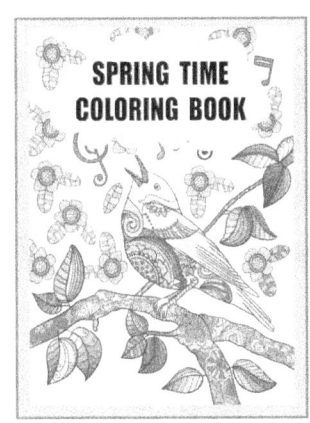

# Color In Fun
# Kids Books

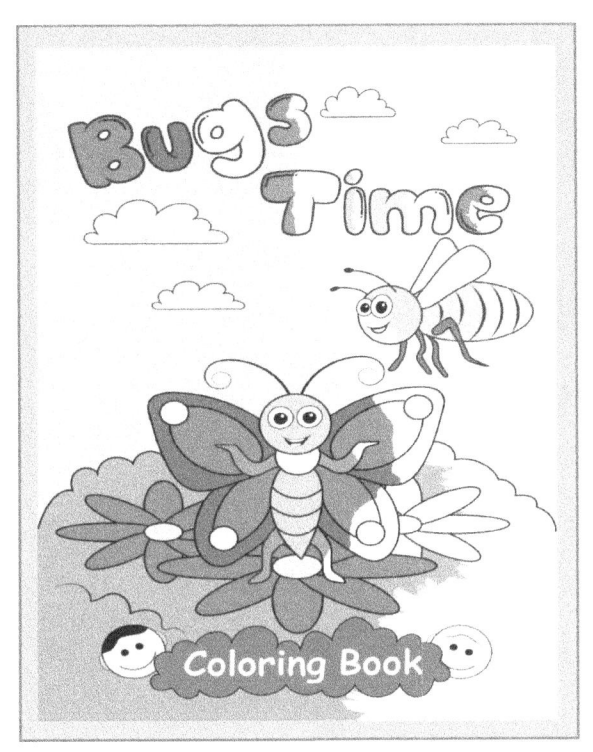

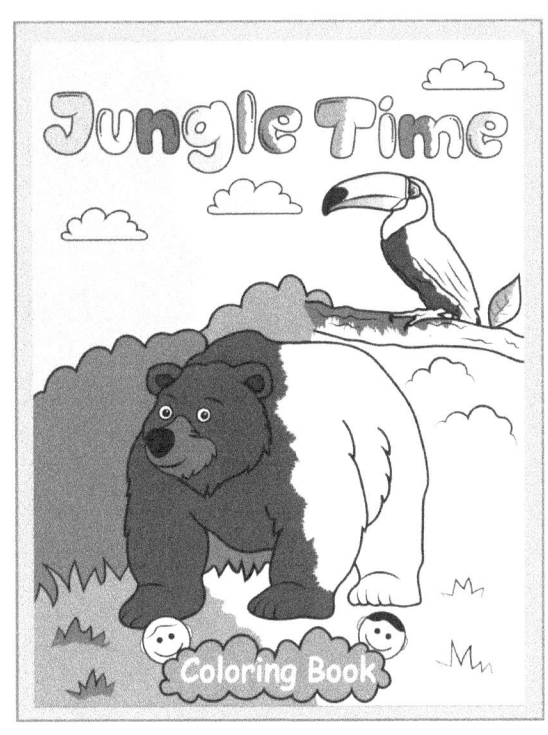

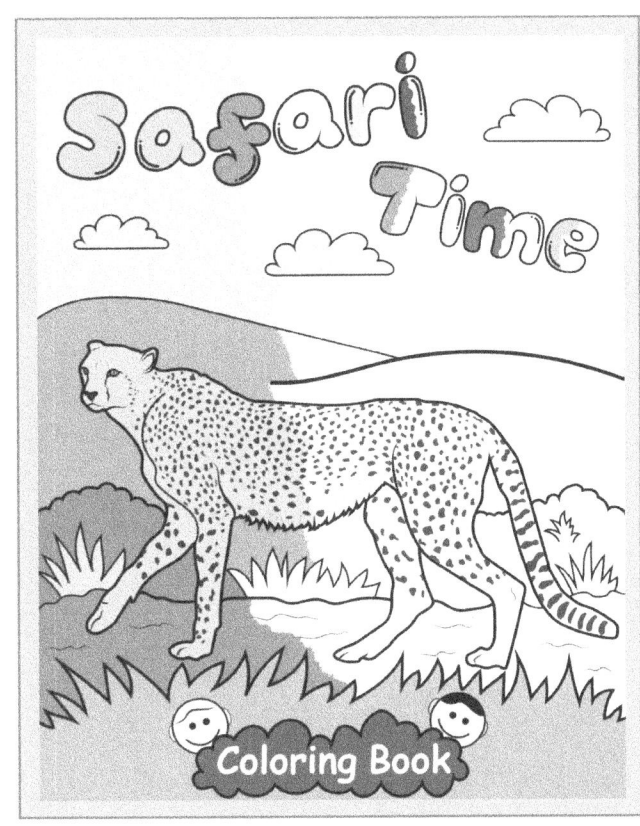

Visit **www.ArylaPublishing.com**
to find out about all new releases.

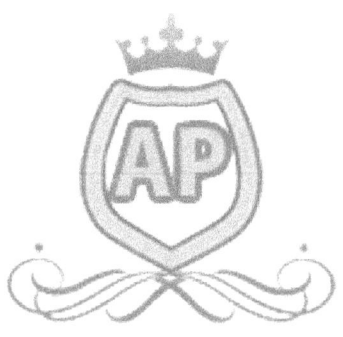

Follow us @arylapublishing on Twitter Instagram & Facebook

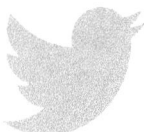  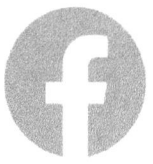

Search for Aryla Publishing on

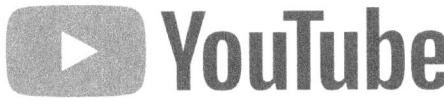 YouTube

**Check out our <u>Book Trailers</u>**

<u>Subscribe</u> **to keep up to date with new releases!**

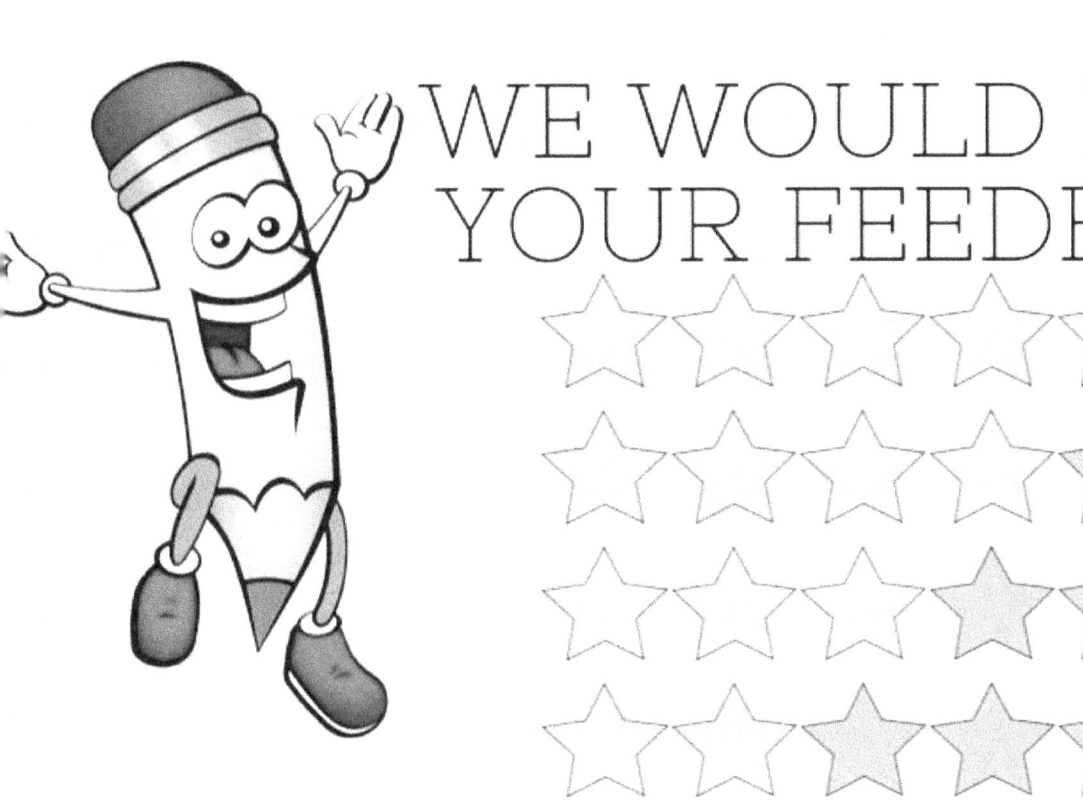

# WE WOULD LOVE YOUR FEEDBACK

**PLEASE LEAVE REVIEW AT:-**

https://viewbook.at/undertheseareview

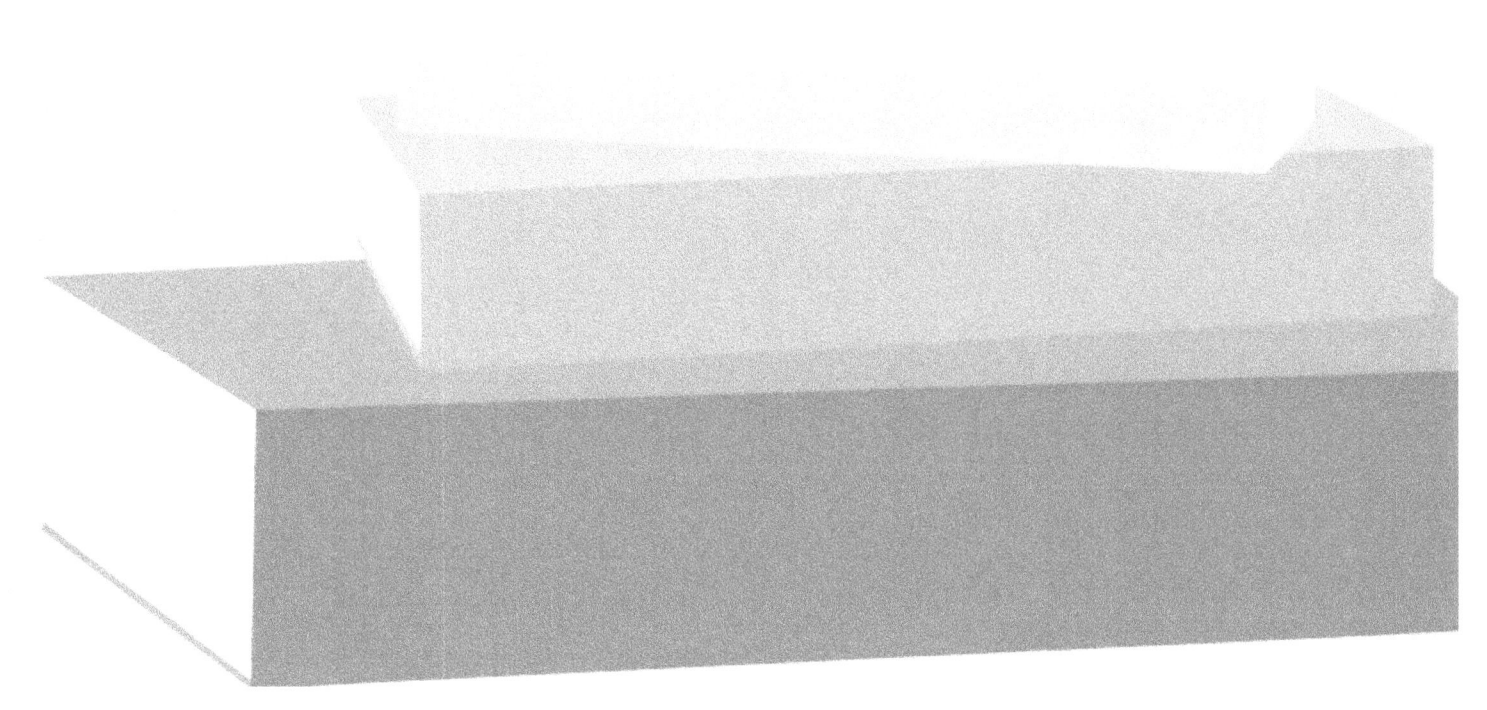

www.ingramcontent.com/pod-product-compliance
Lightning Source LLC
Chambersburg PA
CBHW080134240526

45468CB00009BA/2436